FINANCIAL FREEDOM ON $5 A DAY

FINANCIAL FREEDOM ON $5 A DAY

Chuck Chakrapani, M.Sc., Ph.D., C.I.M.

Self-Counsel Press
(a division of)
International Self-Counsel Press Ltd
USA   Canada

First edition: March 1983
Second edition: February 1984
Third edition: January 1986; Reprinted: September 1986
Fourth edition: March 1989
Fifth edition: April 1991; Reprinted: July 1991; May 1992; September 1993
Sixth edition: December 1994; Reprinted: September 1995; February 1996
Seventh edition: May 1999

Canadian Cataloguing in Publication Data
Chakrapani, Chuck
Financial freedom on $5 a day

(Self-counsel business series)
ISBN 1-55180-231-7
ISSN 0827-2522
1. Investments — Periodicals. 2. Speculation — Periodicals.
I. Title. II. Series.
HG4527.C428   332.6'78   C84-031650-X

Self-Counsel Press
(*a division of*)
International Self-Counsel Press Ltd.

1704 N. State Street	1481 Charlotte Road
Bellingham, WA 98225	North Vancouver, BC V7J 1H1
USA	Canada

CONTENTS

PART III: HOW TO INVEST: PROFIT OPPORTUNITIES FOR THE SMALL INVESTOR

CHARTS

SAMPLES

PREFACE

This book describes a safe, long-term investment strategy. Even if you have no savings at the moment, even if you can save no more than $5 a day, you can achieve financial freedom using the techniques described in this book.

Most books on investing assume that you have several thousand dollars to invest. Unfortunately, this is not always true. Many of us do not have large savings. It is not easy to get investment advice when you do not have several thousand dollars to invest. Many investment advisers will not take the time to explain what you should do with your $300. There are no books on the market that will explain the options open to you.

This book is different. It tells you how you can invest, starting with as little as $100. The information is very specific. The book gives you the addresses and phone numbers of companies you can contact. It explains specific investments and tells you how you can get a piece of the action. In this edition of the book, I have updated information and rewritten some chapters.

Inevitably, there is a gap between the time the information is collected and the time it eventually reaches you. Therefore, no matter how much I have tried to make the book up-to-date, there will be some addresses and phone numbers that are out of date. If you are unsuccessful with a few addresses or phone numbers, don't be discouraged. There is enough information in this book to create your investment plan — a plan that will make you financially independent, slowly but surely.

This book does not distinguish between the Canadian and the U.S. dollar. Items that refer to the U.S. market are in U.S. dollars and items that refer to the Canadian market are in Canadian dollars. If you need $100 to join a U.S. mutual fund you need U.S. $100; if you need $100 to join a Canadian mutual fund you need Cdn. $100. Prices of gold and silver are, by tradition, in U.S. dollars.

The first edition of this book came out in 1983. Since then I have received hundreds of letters from readers telling me how useful they have found it. The information in this book takes a long time to compile and such letters make me feel that this project is worthwhile. Thank you.

The amount of research that goes into a book of this nature requires the help of several people. It is impossible to thank everyone individually. However, one person deserves special thanks: Christine Mole, who assisted me in every way in putting together this edition of the book.

I have written more than ten books. But *Financial Freedom on $5 a Day* gives me the greatest satisfaction. Basic books on investing have a notoriously short life. So it pleases me to note that, with your support, this book has been continuously in print for more than 15 years.

Most authors look for endorsement of their work from celebrities and famous people. To me, the most meaningful endorsement comes from my readers. They have read it, used it, and found that it delivers what it claims. I would like to quote just two letters out of the hundreds in our files. (These are unsolicited testimonials written by readers; the originals can be viewed at the Standard Research Systems offices by appointment.)

> At 45, after 20 years of marriage, we had no savings, no investments....Sixty days after buying your book I have $700 split between

two investments and $1,000 in savings. The "Ten Plus Principle" alone was worth the cash of the book many times over. Thank you! Thank you!

Mrs. N.K., West Palm Beach, Florida

I bought your book in the early eighties when I was broke. Then I started saving $5 a day from your ideas in the book. I saved enough to buy a duplex for $35,000... We put $10,000 into the property, now it is worth $150,000. I paid my mortgage off in 1989 and bought my second home on the St. Lawrence River for $90,000. Now after two years of hard work, it is worth $175,000... I have just bought your new book for myself and my son and am looking for new ways of investing. Thanks! Your book was a great help to me and other people I have helped with saving money.

Mr. J.E. Brockville, Ontario

I do not want to pretend that I wrote this book for purely altruistic reasons. Among other things, I am an author by profession. But one of my motives for writing this book is to help small investors who cannot get such help elsewhere. It pleases me a great deal to know that it made a difference in a few people's lives and they cared to share it with me.

I hope it makes a difference in your life and I wish you the very best.

PART I
FINANCIAL FREEDOM:
YOU CAN ACHIEVE IT

1
YOU CAN ACHIEVE
FINANCIAL FREEDOM

a. EVEN SMALL INVESTORS CAN ACHIEVE FINANCIAL FREEDOM

What if I told you that within a year from today you could have:

- investments in the stock market,
- investments in bonds,
- international investments,
- some gold and silver,
- equity in real estate,

and much more? Would you believe it?

Whether you believe it or not, you can have all these and even more. All you need to do is put the ideas described in this book into practice. Many people have already done it. I have had many letters from people who read earlier editions of this book and put into practice what they read. Many of them started with practically no savings. Yet, by now, they are financially independent. Or they are on their way to becoming so.

The ideas presented are simple but powerful. There are no gimmicks in this book. Instead, you will find many no-nonsense ideas regarding investments that have high profit potential.

You have probably always suspected that there are highly profitable investments open to the small investor. But

3

how can you find out about them? After all, most investment advisers are after big money. They are not interested in telling you how to wisely invest your first $100.

The result? Most small investors remain in the dark about the opportunities open to them. Small investors continue to be small investors, while large investors continue to increase their wealth.

Help is on the way! This book is written to show you how to build wealth, even if you don't have any savings now. North America is still a land of opportunities. If you ever dream about becoming financially free, your dream can become reality.

Several years ago when I started investing, no one told me that wonderful opportunities existed for the small investor. I wasted many years pursuing useless advice. Investment books provided little usable advice for the small investor.

If you are in the same position as I was several years ago, let me assure you, you are much better off than I was. You hold in your hands a book that tells you:

- how to set up an investment program that does not require mountains of cash to start

- how to begin today — not after you have saved enough money to invest. A book that takes the mystery out of investing and makes investing understandable and fun!

- how to set up a successful investment program that works automatically and with little or no risk

- how to be your own financial consultant so you understand and manage your money

I know that the principles contained in this book, simple as they may be, work. They have worked for me and they have worked for many people over the years.

b. WHY AREN'T MOST PEOPLE FINANCIALLY INDEPENDENT?

Most people in our society would like to be financially independent, but unfortunately most of us are not. If, as I believe, North America is still a place of opportunities, why aren't most of us financially independent?

I know we can all be financially independent. I will prove it to you by the time you finish reading this book. For the time being, just assume that anyone who wants to be financially free can be. Then why aren't most people financially independent? Why can't about 95% of North Americans fully support themselves when they retire?

The reason is simple. We all want the good life. But we are not prepared to do what it takes to achieve it. *Doing whatever it takes to get there is the secret of success,* in investing as in life. It is unfortunate that most people do not do what it takes to achieve financial freedom. Most people don't realize this, but what you need to do is simple and straightforward. As this book suggests, start today with $5, put aside $5 every day, add to it as time goes on, and invest wisely. That is all it takes.

Yet most of us do not do what it takes to get to financial independence. We hope. We procrastinate. We hesitate. We wait for the magic day when we will have the "money to invest." When we invest, we do so on the spur of the moment with no rhyme or reason. We do not start with a plan.

To achieve financial freedom you need a plan. You are unlikely to achieve financial freedom by random investments or by daydreaming. Even hard work may not get you there. Just as you cannot hope to end up with a house by building walls without a plan, so you cannot hope to achieve financial freedom without a plan. Many investors do not achieve financial freedom because they work without a plan — they are simply building walls hoping that somehow they will end up with a house!

5

c. WHAT IT TAKES TO ACHIEVE FINANCIAL FREEDOM

Achieving financial freedom is not difficult. As I said earlier, anyone who wants it can achieve it. There are, in fact, four ingredients to financial success. They are:

(a) Regular savings, however small

(b) Patience and avoidance of greed

(c) A well-conceived plan of action

(d) Knowing where and how to invest

If you can look after the first two items, this book will assist you with the last two items: a plan of action and information on where and how to invest your money for healthy profits.

Investments should have a purpose. They should be made regularly. You need patience and you should avoid greed. Why are these things important? Without a purpose, you cannot make logical investment choices. Without patience, you may abandon your program halfway through. With greed, you are likely to lose all your money in some absurd scheme to get rich quickly. Avoid these traps. In fact, if you simply follow this book faithfully, you will automatically avoid these traps.

Will reading this book make you financially independent? Reading this book, or any other book for that matter, will not make you financially independent — unless you act upon its suggestions. It is not knowledge but *action* that makes people successful. To succeed, you should be prepared to put the principles described in this book into practice.

I have tried to make it easier for you to act on my suggestions. When I ask you to save, I discuss how to save. When I suggest that you consider a particular investment, I have included contact addresses and phone numbers. When

6

I say you should find out more, I have listed what you should read. In fact, this book contains practically everything you need to know. I hope that this book will take you from wherever you are now to financial freedom.

But — and I cannot emphasize this strongly enough — whether you become financially independent or not will depend not on whether you read this book, but on your motivation to act on the suggestions it contains.

The program explained in this book requires your involvement and commitment for you to succeed. With your involvement and commitment, you are on your way to financial freedom. Can you pay yourself $5 a day to start and spend 30 minutes a month reviewing your investments? If you can, it is virtually certain that you will achieve financial freedom in the next few years.

d. DREAM MERCHANTS: DO YOU WANT TO PAY THEM?

The world of investing is full of dream merchants. Out in the world are many people who are desperate to help you — for a small consideration of just a few (or a few hundred) dollars. Their message is the same: "Give me some money *now* and I will tell you how to get rich *later*." In various forms, here are their messages:

- Start a mail order business with no capital.

- Buy real estate with no money down.

- Buy the stocks I suggest and multiply your money.

- Buy gold futures, pork bellies, or whatever.

- Use pyramid schemes and get rich in 30 days.

These are the conservative ones! The more extreme ones tell you how to pick the winning number in a lottery, buy coins and paintings (that *they* sell), play blackjack, use a "surefire" betting system, think rich, or get involved in a chain letter scheme.

Do they work?

I don't know of anyone who got rich by using a system to pick winning numbers in a lottery. If indeed there were such a system, why are they trying to sell it to us instead of using it themselves so they can spend the rest of their lives getting tanned under the sun by the sea?

Chain letters (which are generally illegal) can make you money if *you* start them and have the good fortune to find a number of gullible people to go along with the scheme. I hope you don't get arrested before you get rich!

In general, you shouldn't be learning the secrets of getting rich from someone who is desperate to let you in on the secret for $10. It is more likely that the money you pay will pay someone else's grocery bills rather than make you rich.

How about the more respectable schemes?

You can indeed make money in the mail order business. But it is hard work and success is by no means guaranteed. Besides, despite claims to the contrary, you will need some capital. While the mail order business has several advantages, it can be tough. It is unrealistic to expect it to be easy to make money in the mail order business. I know — I have sold several items through the mail.

You can also make money in real estate — but not necessarily with ease. Perhaps you know of people who got hurt speculating in real estate. I do.

There are many people in both the mail order and the real estate business who never got rich and probably never will. In any case, despite the extravagant claims of the advertisements, these businesses are not really get-rich-quick schemes. They are legitimate businesses with high profit potential. The qualities to succeed in these ventures are similar to the ones you would need to succeed in any other business — hard work, sufficient capital, and perseverance.

So what's left?

One could speculate on gold or oil (for example, by buying gold in the futures market). Such schemes can work. But what happens to your money will depend on what the gnomes of Zurich and the Saddam Husseins of this world decide to do. For example, if you bought gold futures in early 1979 (and pyramided the profits), you would have become a millionaire by 1980. But if you had bought gold futures in 1980 and pyramided the profits, you would have probably gone bankrupt. Again, you would have made virtually no money by speculating in oil prices in 1989, but you could have made spectacular profits if you had started speculating (in the right direction) in 1990, just before Iraq invaded Kuwait.

Some get-rich-quick schemes work and some don't. Those that do, do not work consistently. Many schemes carry a high level of risk. It is my view that get-rich-quick schemes are simply not suitable for most investors — whether large or small, beginning or sophisticated. It is better to get rich slowly than to get poor in a hurry.

e. GETTING RICH SLOWLY BUT SURELY

Now that we have dismissed get-rich-quick schemes, can a small investor, starting with no capital, really get rich? The answer is yes. Any investor can make enough money to become financially free. It takes discipline, patience, and a little effort. And it takes time. But it can be done. If you have enough money to buy this book and if you are sincerely willing to put what is described into practice, you probably have all it takes to achieve financial freedom!

The techniques described in this book will not make you rich overnight. But they will lead you to financial freedom in the next few years. As I said earlier, you need a certain amount of patience, discipline, and effort. This does not mean

9

that you have to sacrifice your present happiness to achieve future financial freedom. Slightly rewording *Alice in Wonderland*, what we need is jam today *and* jam tomorrow!

It is meaningless to suffer today so you can be happy sometime in the future. Today is as important as any other day of your life. The program in this book is designed in such a way that you can carry it out without feeling that you have to forego the essential things you need now.

You will need some discipline, but let me assure you, it will not cramp your style! After all, you are not likely to achieve financial freedom if you do not plan and if you are unwilling to change your habits a bit. Getting rich does not demand that we make ourselves miserable now. It does mean, however, that we make some gentle changes in the way we spend and save.

Although the program described here will work for all types of investors, I have designed it specially for investors who —

- do not want to start and run a business,

- believe that there is no such thing as a free lunch,

- do not want to take undue risks with their money, and

- would rather invest $10 wisely than pay hundreds of dollars for a get-rich-quick scheme.

f. IS IT STILL $5 A DAY?

It is over 15 years since this book first came out. With all the inflation since then, are we still talking about $5 a day? Should we increase it to *Financial Freedom on $10 a Day*? Here is the good news: it is still $5 a day!

What stops most people from achieving financial freedom is the idea that they have to have a lot of money to get started. So start with any amount. Five dollars a day is good enough.

If you can't afford even that, start with even less. See for yourself how easy it is to build an investment plan and how well your money grows. Once you have done that, you will find ways to increase your daily investment to the extent you can afford. If you stick with the plan even for a couple of years, you will begin to see the results you like. By then, you will be thinking of new ways to save and invest. You will not be finding excuses to avoid investing.

g. FIVE DOLLARS A DAY GETS YOU STARTED

Financial freedom on $5 a day! Is it possible? The answer is yes and I will show you how.

Let's say that you are now 30 years old and that you plan to retire at 65. If you can save just $5 a day and invest for a 13% return, you will have well over $1,200,000 by the time you retire — even if you have no other savings and no other investment plan.

But of course you want to be financially independent long before you retire — unless you are already close to retirement. And it can be done. The point of the example is simply to show that you do not have to start with a lot of money to retire financially independent.

If you are willing to set aside a small amount each day, and if you are willing to be patient, you can achieve financial freedom. This book will show you how.

The program described in this book will work for you even if you do not know anything about investments, and even if you do not have a lot of savings now. I am assuming, however, that you are willing to be systematic and patient with your investments and will take the initiative to implement the program. Let's get busy! Five dollars a day gets you started. Today is the day to begin.

2
WHAT MAKES YOU WEALTHY?

a. WHAT IS FINANCIAL FREEDOM ANYWAY?

Financial freedom means different things to different people. For me, it means maintaining my current lifestyle through my investments without having to depend on other sources of income. Suppose you make $40,000 a year. Financial freedom is when you can make about $40,000 a year solely through your investments. If you can accumulate a capital of about $333,000 and invest it for an average return of 12%, then you will get $40,000 a year.

If you are sufficiently interested in putting the principles in this book into practice, chances are that you will be able to achieve financial freedom. The basic premise of the book is this: most people, regardless of their current situation, can achieve financial freedom. There might be obvious exceptions. If you are already 63 and have no savings but would like to achieve financial freedom by 65, it is unlikely that this book will make it happen. On the other hand, if you are in your early forties or even your fifties, and you are willing to make up for lost time, there is no reason why you cannot achieve financial freedom or something close to it.

Financial freedom is not a "yes" or "no" condition. If you need $40,000 of investment income, but can make only $35,000 a year through your investments, you are still much better off than someone who is entirely at the mercy of government and private pensions.

So here it is. *The principles laid out in this book will help most people achieve financial freedom, regardless of their current situation.*

You may be tempted to say that you are too close to retirement, or that you are already retired, or that you have heavy personal debts. Even in these cases, I believe that putting the principles described in this book into practice will make your financial situation better than it would be otherwise.

b. HOW DO I GET THERE FROM HERE?

Maybe you are still skeptical. You are probably wondering how, starting from scratch, you can go from zero wealth to financial freedom. After all, in the first chapter I dismissed all get-rich-quick schemes as being unsuitable for small investors. In fact, I even suggested that you should avoid risking your money in your search for a higher return. If I say there are no magical solutions and if I don't promise you the moon, you may wonder how you are ever going to achieve financial freedom. Especially when I say that all you need to begin with is just $5 a day.

You have a right to be skeptical, and I hope you are. Skepticism is the best protection an investor has against the sharks that infest the sea of investment.

c. THREE POWERFUL PRINCIPLES

The program that I am about to describe incorporates three powerful principles of investing. These principles are powerful, though they may look deceptively simple.

1. The magic of compounding

If you invest $1,000 at 12% interest per year, you will have $2,000 in 6 years. But if you leave it for about 30 years, you will have $30,000 if you don't add a penny during all that time. During the first 6 years, your investment made only $1,000. But between the years 24 and 30, your investment made $15,000. When you invest, your money will grow faster and faster as time goes on. This is because money makes money, and the money that money makes, makes even more money. This is the magic of compounding. The

Financial Freedom on $5 a Day strategy (3FD strategy for short) is a long-term strategy that takes full advantage of the principle of compounding.

One of the major mistakes in investing is made by young people. Nobody told them about the power of compound interest. So they postpone investing to some future date. This is a major mistake.

Let me illustrate. Joe invests $2,000 a year between the ages of 18 and 23 and does not invest any further. Jane starts at age 25 and invests $2,000 every year until her retirement at age 65. (Assume a return of 10% in both cases.) Who will have more money when they retire? Jane? Guess again.

Believe it or not, Joe's $10,000 investment would be worth $735,600 at retirement while Jane's $42,000 would be worth $531,111 — just because Joe had a few more years' compound return than Jane.

You are never too young to start investing. In fact, you can achieve spectacular returns if you start early, and the earlier the better.

But neither are you too old to start investing. Our strategy will work for anybody who wants to invest to build a secure future. Chart #1 shows how $5 a day would grow over an extended period of time.

2. Dollar cost averaging

Suppose you decide to buy an investment that goes up and down in price. Further, you decide to invest $100 every month on this investment. If the price of this investment for a given month is $10, you will buy 10 units ($100/$10). If the price for the following month is $12.50, you will buy only 8 units ($100/$12.50). If the price drops to $5, then you will buy 20 units ($100/$5). In other words, by investing the same amount every month, you buy more when the price is low and less when the price is high. In most situations, your

CHART #1
FUTURE VALUE — $150 SAVED MONTHLY
13% interest compounded monthly

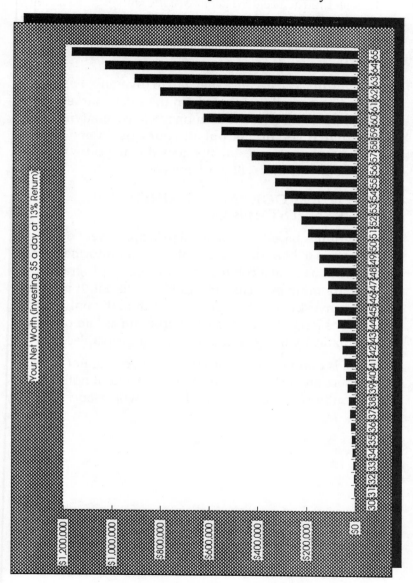

average price will turn out to be lower than what it would have been if you had not used this method.

This technique is called *dollar cost averaging.* The strategy described in this book incorporates the dollar cost averaging technique.

3. Diversification

Many investors lose because they fail to diversify. For example, they may put all their money in the stock market. If the market crashes, they lose their money. By diversifying, you make sure that you do not put all your eggs in one basket. Even if one of your investments goes down, you will have other investments that will work for you.

d. USE THE PROGRAM TO MONITOR YOUR INVESTMENTS

This program is based on powerful principles, yet you don't have to spend a lot of time setting it up or monitoring it. It is simple. You may have come across automatic programs before that are mindless. This program is different. It is based on sound investment principles. It is automatic only in the sense that as long as you follow the program as laid out, you are automatically using sound investment principles.

There is nothing in this program that you cannot understand. There are no black boxes. You need accept nothing on faith or authority. You will see how it works and why it works.

PART II
GETTING MONEY TO INVEST

3
HOW TO GET MONEY TO INVEST

a. PAY YOURSELF FIRST

Do you tell yourself that you will start saving and investing when you earn more? Many people do. Years go by, but the day never arrives. Their income has increased over the years, but so have their expenditures. They say to themselves that they will start saving when they earn even more! When they are about to retire, they wonder what they did with all their money over the years!

Simply put, if you wait for your income to increase before you start saving, you will probably never make it. You have to start saving now.

Today.

But how? How can you possibly save when you have no money left by the end of the month?

Wait a minute. You work hard for your money. You take care of all your bills — telephone, hydro, rent, household expenses, gifts. The list goes on. But did you pay yourself? When you have paid all your bills, what have you got left for yourself? Nothing? You have nothing to show for all your hard work? Are you saying that money simply passes through your hands and you have no control over it?

How can this be? I know how. Most people tend to plan backwards. Instead of paying themselves first, they pay others first. Then they find that there is nothing left.

This way of thinking has to change. Now. As Northcote Parkinson said, expenditure rises to meet income. This is why

19

you find that although your income has risen over the years, you have no significant savings. That is what is wrong in believing that at some future time you will be able save, but not now.

If you want to achieve financial independence, the first commandment is PAY YOURSELF FIRST. The amount you pay yourself may be small (like $5 a day), but you have to pay yourself first. When you pay yourself, you will automatically begin to adjust your other expenses.

"Easier said than done!" you may say. But think of the alternative. You have a choice. You can pay yourself first and look forward to a secure future or you can find excuses to avoid paying yourself and look forward to being strapped in your old age.

Let me assure you that there are simple and painless ways of saving. I describe them in the next section.

b. THREE SIMPLE WAYS TO SAVE

Different people save differently. In my opinion, there are three ways to save that are particularly simple. You can save by using any one of these three techniques:

(a) The Minus Ten technique

(b) The Plus Ten technique

(c) The Day's Due technique

You can use any method that appeals to you.

1. The Minus Ten technique

When you use this method, you arrange to have 10% of your salary deducted before it reaches you. For example, you can instruct your bank or trust company to transfer 10% of your salary every month to a (different) savings account. As far as you are concerned, the remaining 90% left in your regular account is all that is available for spending.

The 10% that is transferred to a different account is not your spending money, it is not your emergency money, it is not your holiday money — it is your investment money, the money that will make you financially independent.

2. The Plus Ten technique

This is my favorite technique. Whenever you spend money, set aside 10% of the money spent. For example, if you spend $500 on rent, set aside $50 toward saving. If you spend $1 on coffee, set aside a dime. Do this no matter how small or how large the expenditure is. Develop your "Plus Ten" thinking. This way, you'll automatically add 10% to all items; it is like adding your own tax so that you can be financially independent. If you want to buy an item that costs $100, think of it as costing you $110. That is the amount you need to buy the item. If you don't have it, you can't afford it! This is an easy way to save, because you are forced to save whenever you spend. If you don't want to save, don't spend!

There is another advantage to this method. Because you have to save every time you spend, you have to pay attention to your spending. Paying attention to spending can make you aware of unnecessary and mechanical spending.

Each week you should deposit all the money you saved using the "Plus Ten" method into a separate savings account.

3. Day's Due technique

Decide on an amount that you can comfortably save each day. Although in this book I suggest a minimum of $5 a day, if you can start with only $3 a day — even $1 a day — start with that amount. Consistency is important. You have to save every day — Saturdays, Sundays, holidays — no exceptions.

What is the ideal amount to save every day? As I said, it depends on your personal situation. You can start with $5 a day or even $1 a day. But the ideal minimum amount you should save is:

Your annual salary ÷ 3,500

For example, if your annual salary is $35,000, you should aim to save:

$35,000 ÷ 3,500 = $10 a day.

If your annual salary is $70,000, you should aim to save $20 a day. To begin with, it does not matter what the exact amount is. But once you decide on an amount, make sure that you save that amount each day.

No matter which of the three methods you use, make sure that your savings are deposited in a separate savings account until it is time to invest. This money should not be used for any other purpose — not even in an emergency. It has been repeatedly observed that when we use this money for an emergency, soon another emergency will arise and then another emergency and then another emergency. Besides, how are we going to replace the money once we take it out? Make sure that the money you need for holidays, emergencies, and other contingencies is kept separate from your investment account.

c. AIM TO SAVE AT LEAST 10% OF YOUR INCOME

Each of the three methods described in the previous section will help you to save a minimum of 10% of your income. In my view, anyone who is seriously interested in becoming financially free should aim to save at least this much. While you can start with a smaller amount, if your savings fall below 10%, it will take you longer to achieve financial independence.

Some people may feel that they cannot possibly save 10% of their income. They should ask themselves the following question: If you cannot live on 90% of your income today, how will you get by when you retire, when your income is likely to be just one-half or one-third of your current income?

Start with $1 a day. Or $5 a day. But always aim to save at least 10% of your income. Once you make it a habit, you won't find it hard at all.

It is very important that you *do not attempt to start with an amount that is too high. You must be certain that you can keep saving at this level.* This is your first priority. Your next priority is to increase your savings to 10% of your income or higher over a period of time, even if you cannot do it right away.

d. SIX WAYS TO RAISE ADDITIONAL MONEY FOR INVESTING

If you don't have any savings now (or even if you do) you may still raise additional money for investing. My long-time friend and best-selling author, William E. Donoghue, describes six methods in his interesting book, *Guide to Finding Money to Invest*:

1. Liberate the lemons

Perhaps you have cash in various forms that is not working for you. For example, you may have some traveler's checks and foreign currency left over from your previous holiday. You may have more money in a low-interest-paying account than you need right now. Consolidate all such cash.

Next, go through your house room by room. Collect every item you don't like or you have not used for several months (including your clothes). Be ruthless. Organize a garage sale and sell everything you no longer use.

2. Slash your major expenses

You can cut your payments in many ways. You can cut your insurance payments by choosing the right type of insurance that will fit your needs rather than the most expensive one available. You can cut your total mortgage payments substantially by using techniques such as prepaying part of the principal or increasing the frequency of payments. You can discontinue subscriptions to magazines you hardly ever read. In fact, if you analyze your lifestyle, you may find various ways of slashing your major expenses.

3. Squeeze your budget

The trick is to squeeze your budget without getting squashed. You need to learn the art of creative scrimping. Like banking at an institution whose service charges are lower. Like buying seasonal vegetables which are likely to be fresh and less expensive than out of season produce. Don't just buy your usual choices out of habit.

4. Reduce your taxes

Or as Donoghue puts it, "reduce the thighs of your tax bill with accounting aerobics." For example, your employer may be deducting a larger than necessary amount towards taxes. Have your employer reduce your tax deduction so you have the use of your money now, rather than when you get it back from the government. Are you sure that you are claiming all the deductions you are eligible for? If not, read a good book on the subject to find out what deductions you are eligible for.

5. Increase your return without risk

Take another look at the money you have in your savings account. Can you earn a higher rate of interest at another financial institution? After all, your money is insured up to a certain amount in most institutions. As long as there is no higher risk, why not get a higher rate of return on your savings?

6. Adopt friction-free investing

Friction costs are those that you pay as commissions and loads. If you are a small investor, it is particularly important that your money supports only your investments and not someone else's lifestyle. Wherever possible, adopt friction-free investing — use discount brokers and mutual funds that charge no commission. More on this topic later.

If you cannot find any extra money even using these techniques, remember that saving $5 a day will give you $100 in three weeks' time.

7. Watch those windfalls

From time to time we all get extra money — often unexpectedly. It could be your bonus, or a tax refund or inheritance of some type, or even a small lottery winning. You should *always* save something out of every windfall. I suggest that you attempt to save at least 50% out of every windfall. If you keep adding unexpected gains to your investment program, you will reach your goal of financial freedom much sooner.

e. BUILDING AN INVESTMENT PYRAMID

All investments are not equally powerful. Some investments carry high returns and others carry low returns. Generally speaking, investments that carry high rewards tend to be risky; investments that carry low rewards tend to be less risky.

What should a small investor do? If you choose a high-return investment, it is likely to carry a higher degree of risk so that you could lose a part or all of your capital. If you choose a low-risk investment, your return will be low and you may have to wait a long time to become financially free.

To know what you should do, you should first list your objectives. I suggest that your objectives at this stage should be the following:

- Very important — Safety of your capital

- Important — High return

- Highly desirable — Potentially very high return

For a conservative investor, safety of capital is of paramount importance. Why? To win the investment game, *you need to be in the game*. Once you lose your capital, you are not in the game any more. That is why preserving your capital is so important. It is so important that, to have this security, you must be willing to accept a lower rate of return at the initial stages of investing. However, as you invest more and more actively, you may want to risk a small part of your capital for a chance to win big. Sooner or later, all investors have to take some risks if they are to win big. As you start investing wisely, you will learn the difference between calculated risks and wishful thinking. Until you develop a feel for calculated risks, you should err on the cautious side.

A standard technique to achieve balance in your investments is known as the investment pyramid (see figure).

As a small investor, you need to protect your investments. Therefore, the bulk of your investments should be in low-risk, above-average return investments. This forms the base for your investment pyramid. Once the base is secure, you may want to add investments that carry average risk but above-average return. Once you have both of these types of investments, you may venture into the top of the pyramid with high-risk investments that give you an opportunity to make very high returns — if you are successful.

How much should you invest in each of the three types of investments? It depends on several factors. If you are young, you can afford to take more risks than if you are near retirement. If you are a risk-taker by nature, you may want to invest more on risky investments than if you are risk-averse by nature. A small investor is less likely to be in a position to take risks compared to a large investor.

No matter what level of risk you prefer, please remember the concept of the *pyramid*. Put more money in safe investments and less money in risky investments. This rule applies to all investors.

A broad guideline for building an investment pyramid is as follows:

- Low-risk investments: 50% to 70%
- Average-risk investments: 30% to 40%
- High-risk investments: 0% to 10%

You can change the guideline to suit your needs, but make sure that you start with a philosophy of investing. In other words, decide beforehand what is best for you. Buy only those investments that are in line with your objectives.

f. RULES OF SUCCESS FOR THE SMALL INVESTOR

The game of investing has rules. However, the rules are not the same for everyone. A small investor will have a different set of rules than a large investor. A young investor will have a different set of rules than an older investor. If you are in a high tax bracket, you will have a different set of rules than if you are in a low tax bracket. We will consider here only those rules that are useful for the small investor. Three rules are particularly useful.

1. Save regularly

If you are a small investor, you cannot afford to be irregular in your savings. Discipline is an essential part of successful investing. Once you commit yourself to save a particular amount you should stick to it. You should not make any exceptions. From time to time an unforeseen expenditure may come up for which you need money. You might be tempted to skip saving that day (or month). Don't. Why? Because it has been repeatedly observed that:

> *If, at any time, an unexpected expenditure comes up and you fail to save because of it, another unexpected expenditure will arise in the near future. Such unexpected expenditures will keep arising over and over again until your savings program falls apart.*

Therefore, small investors should make no exceptions to their savings routine. Weekends, holidays, days when you are not well — none of these should make any difference. Because you shouldn't make exceptions, you should set up a realistic program. Do not be overambitious and commit yourself to saving 25% of your salary, if you cannot realistically carry on the program for any length of time. Let me emphasize again: it is very important that you be consistent with your program; the amount you save is important, but not nearly as important as consistency and discipline.

2. Invest for maximum return

You might have heard — or even noticed — that the rich get richer and the poor get poorer. There is some truth to this maxim. Not only are the rich better off to begin with, they get better deals compared to the poor. Let us compare a small and a large investor:

(a) *A small investor is likely to pay a higher commission compared to a large investor.* For example, if you buy $500 worth of shares, you could be charged the maximum commission which could be 10% of your investment. A large investor who buys $10,000 worth of shares (of the same stock) will probably pay a commission of about 2%.

(b) *A small investor is likely to get a lower return compared to a large investor.* For instance, if you invest your money in Guaranteed Investment Certificates (GICs), your return will be higher if you invest a large amount, and lower if you invest a small amount. Some high-return investments (such as commercial papers) are not even open to small investors.

(c) *A small investor's investments are either vulnerable or not highly profitable.* Because small investors have fewer options compared to large investors, small investors are often forced to choose between low-return and high-risk investments.

Such a system which rewards the rich and penalizes the not-so-rich may be unfair, but it is the only system we have. It is not about to change, but take heart. This book will show how a small investor can invest *nearly as profitably as a rich investor.* There are many opportunities open to small investors. You'll find out about these opportunities in this book. If you act on these opportunities you will move into the world of high finance, no matter how little you have to invest.

3. Minimize your commissions

I have nothing against commissions. But small investors should be careful as to how they spend their capital. When you pay a large commission on an investment, you have less money to invest.

Suppose you invest $1,000 at 15% a year. If you do not have to pay any commission, you will have $4,045 at the end of ten years. On the other hand, if you have to pay a commission of 6%, you will have only $3,802 at the end of ten years. This is a difference of $243 over the investment period, one quarter of your original investment!

There is also another issue. When you pay a large commission to get into an investment, the salesperson is keenly interested in selling that investment to you. It is in his or her interest to glorify the investment. I am not suggesting all salespeople are unscrupulous. They are not. But it is only human nature to maximize one's personal interests. So it is up to you to look after your own interests.

Of the three requirements, you look after the first one — save regularly and I will show you how to invest for high returns and how to minimize commissions.

Now that we have finished with the preliminaries, let's go straight to discovering how you can invest to achieve financial freedom. The next part of the book describes some specific investments that are available to the small investor. Most of these investments can be bought for $100 or even less.

PART III
HOW TO INVEST:
PROFIT OPPORTUNITIES FOR THE
SMALL INVESTOR

4

GETTING STARTED

a. DOUBLE JEOPARDY

Money talks. When you have a lot of money to begin with, you can get better advice which will help you make even more money. For example, here's what you get for your money if you leave it with your bank for one year:

Amount ($)	One-year interest rate (%)
$500	0.05%
5,000	1.40
10,000	1.75

This is what Canadian banks were paying their customers in fall of 1998.

If you buy one ounce of gold bullion, you probably will pay a small premium — maybe between 3% to 6%. If you buy one gram of bullion, you will pay a minimum premium of 15%. If you buy one bond, the commission costs will be proportionately higher than if you buy ten bonds. Mutual funds that charge a commission ("load") usually reduce it for larger investors — sometimes by nearly 90%.

This is true of practically all investments.

There you have it. Double jeopardy. Small investors don't have much money to begin with *and* they have to pay out proportionately more of their money as commissions and premiums.

Besides, I'll bet if you walked into an investment company with $100,000 to invest they would take the time to sit with you and explain the options. But if you walked in with $100....

Sounds rather unfair, but that's the way it is.

b. INVESTMENTS WITH CLOUT

There is good news, however. There are investments suited to the small investor that have nearly as much clout as large investments.

Why is it that many small investors don't know much about these investments? The reason is simple. Suppose you have only $100 to invest. Even if you pay a hefty commission of 10%, your adviser receives only $10. It is simply not worth the adviser's time. The result is that small investors continue to be small — often they get even smaller.

c. TAKING RESPONSIBILITY

Let me share a secret with you. *You have all you need to succeed in investing.* I call it a secret only because so few seem to be aware of this fact. This book will support you by providing specific information. However, the final responsibility for investing is always yours. Do not invest in anything because I (or anyone else) say so. Your investment decision must make sense to you.

To be successful, you must take responsibility for your investment decisions. When you understand an investment and take responsibility for investing in it, if it fails to work out, you'll know why. You can make a better decision next time. But if you do something blindly because someone else told you so, you will learn nothing — whether your investment does well or not.

From the letters I have received from readers of earlier editions of this book, I know that thousands of people have benefited from the suggestions given. I hope the book will help you too. No matter how helpful the book is, always remember, it is your money and it is your decision.

d. A NOTE ON SPECIFIC INFORMATION

I have tried to put together all the information a small investor needs to know to invest wisely and for the highest return. I have even included the addresses and phone numbers you will need to get started.

1. Names and addresses

I have tried to exclude the names and addresses of those institutions that have an undesirable reputation. But I have no way of checking the hundreds of institutions that are listed here. Please always try to get more information before committing your money to any institution. The purpose of this book is make your search easier. You and only you are responsible for your final decision.

You should also be aware that quite often institutions move to a different address, and companies merge or change their names. There is a gap between the time the book is written and the time you eventually read it. There may also be an occasional error. So if some phone numbers or addresses turn out to be incorrect, don't let that stop you. If you are serious about investing there is enough information here to get you going for the next few years!

2. Tax implications

The second thing you should be aware of is that different investment gains and losses are taxed differently. These rules can be different in the United States and Canada. Because these rules keep changing and depend on your personal situation, I do not discuss them in this book. Tax implications of your investments are important. I don't believe that they can be dealt with in a satisfactory manner in a short book on investing like this one. But that is not our concern just now. Once your program is established and you start making a sizable amount of money, you should make adjustments to your portfolio and seek the advice of a professional if necessary.

3. The United States and Canada

This book is intended for both U.S. and Canadian investors. I refer to Canadian investments in Canadian dollars, and U.S. or international investments (including gold) in U.S. dollars.

e. HOW TO START INVESTING

Your objective is to build an investment pyramid. An investment pyramid consists of several "bricks." Each brick represents $100. If you save $5 a day, you will have $1,825 or about 18 bricks at the end of the year. Your objective is to save as many "bricks" (or units of $100) as possible each year and use them to build an investment pyramid.

Suppose you decided to save $2,100 over the next 12 months. This is equal to 21 "bricks."

First, build an imaginary pyramid of 21 bricks as shown:

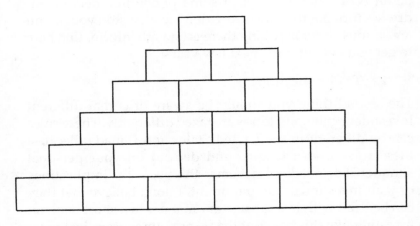

AN INVESTMENT PYRAMID WITH 21 BRICKS

Second, read through the rest of the book and decide how much you want to invest in each type of investment described. As soon as you save $100, immediately invest it according to your plan. Continue to follow your plan as you save more money. If you get some additional money unexpectedly (such as a tax refund or bonus), you may be able to build your pyramid faster than you had anticipated.

Once you have finished building one pyramid, review what you have. If you are happy with what you have, you can start building another pyramid. Repeat the procedure until you achieve financial freedom. In chapter 19 I will discuss how this approach can lead you to financial freedom.

5

HOW TO GET HIGH INTEREST

Your first priority is to protect your capital and make it grow.
You have started your program of saving $5 a day. After less
than three weeks you will have $100. What should you do
with your first $100?

You can leave it in a bank account. But this is not a very
smart idea. You are unlikely to get a high interest rate.
Therefore, you should seek ways of getting a higher rate of
interest than you would if you just left your money in an
account with your bank (or trust company or Savings and
Loan [S&L]).

a. HOW LARGE INVESTORS GET
HIGHER INTEREST RATES

As you might have guessed, large investors do not invest
their money to get the same rate as a savings account earns.
They look for much higher returns and get them.

How do large investors get a higher rate of interest? They
invest in Treasury bills (T-bills). T-bills are a way of lending
money to governments for a short period of time.

Or they buy Certificates of Deposit (CDs). When you buy
CDs, you lend your money to banks for a fixed period.

Or they buy commercial papers. Commercial papers are
a way of lending money to businesses.

The interest rate large investors earn on these investments is much higher than what they would get on a savings
account in a bank — usually 2% to 5% higher. Should interest

rates start moving, the interest rate on the above investments will move up immediately. The interest rate you get on a bank account may or may not move up.

Then why shouldn't we all invest in T-bills, commercial papers, and CDs? Well, there is a snag. Generally speaking, you need $5,000 to $10,000 or even more to take advantage of these opportunities. There is no way a small investor could accumulate such a large amount — at least for a few years. However, there is a way to participate in these investments with only a small amount of money. But one needs to know how.

b. HOW TO GET HIGH INTEREST RATES

To get high interest rates, you may want to join a *money market mutual fund*. What is a money market mutual fund? A money market fund is a pool of money collected from many investors — large and small — and invested in high-yielding T-bills, CDs, and commercial papers. Some of these funds will let you invest $100 or even less! Your small investment will earn an interest rate that is normally available only to large investors.

There are several advantages to investing in money market funds:

- The interest rates are higher (compared to banks, trust companies, or S&Ls).

- Interest rates are compounded daily.

- Most funds charge no commission to join.

- There is no penalty for withdrawal — at any time.

- You can obtain your cash on any working day.

- Some funds — especially in the United States — even let you write checks on your account.

c. HOW TO JOIN A MONEY MARKET FUND

Joining a money market fund is very simple. Just call or write to a money market fund and ask them to send you the details. The information package they send will contain all you need to know to open an account. Pay particular attention to:

- Minimum investment requirement
- Management fee
- Whether they charge a commission (load) to join
- Recent performance

At this stage, you should probably avoid funds that charge a commission to join. Make sure their current return is higher than what you are currently getting on your savings account.

d. NO-LOAD MUTUAL FUNDS

Throughout this book you will hear a lot about no-load mutual funds. A mutual fund collects money from a number of small and large investors and invests it on behalf of the investors. Some of these funds charge a commission that is paid out to the salespeople. Such funds are called "load" funds. Other funds do not have salespeople; they sell the fund units directly to the public. Because they do not have sales-people, they do not charge a commission to invest with them. Such funds are called "no-load funds." Whenever possible, small investors should buy no-load funds, thereby avoiding commission costs. Most of the funds mentioned in this book are no-load.

e. U.S. MONEY MARKET FUNDS

There are literally hundreds of money market funds in the United States. Mutual fund companies as well as several financial institutions offer money market funds. Here are some money market funds based in the United States:

- Benham Tax-Free MMF
- Gabelli US Treasury MMF
- Northwest Treasury Fund
- OLDE Premium Plus MM Series
- Strong Heritage Money Fund
- Strong Municipal MMF
- USAA Tax Exempt CA MMF
- Vanguard Treasury MMF
- Zurich Tax-Free Money Fund

f. CANADIAN MONEY MARKET FUNDS

In Canada, there are over 130 money market funds. Most of them are new. A majority of these funds require an initial investment of at least $1,000 or more. Some funds will accept $500. The funds listed below require only a $100 minimum and are no-load funds. Once you join the fund, they may even accept a lower amount when you add to your initial investment. None of these funds charge a commission to join.

- CDA Money Market Fund
- Co-Operators Money Market Fund
- GWL Money Market (G) NL
- Industrial Alliance Money Market Fund

For more details of all funds listed in this chapter, please refer to the Resource Directory at the end of the book.

g. WHEN TO USE MONEY MARKET FUNDS

Money market funds will give you a better rate of return compared to a savings account. But putting your money in a money market fund is not the best way to get rich. This is because the interest you receive through money market funds is fully taxed. Unless the interest rates are high (as, for example, they were during most of the 1980s), taxes and inflation will cancel out most of your gains. Some of your money can be in money market funds. However, the main use of money market funds is to park your money when you have not yet decided what to do with it.

h. HOW TO EVALUATE THE PERFORMANCE OF YOUR FUND

Before you start investing, you may want to compare the performance of different funds. You may also want to monitor how your fund is doing. Part V, Keeping Track of Your Progress, will show you how.

6

HOW TO INVEST IN STOCKS

Perhaps you have never invested in the stock market. Maybe you wonder what the stock market is, and wonder how you can make money investing in stocks. Even if you are an absolute beginner, you will find this chapter helpful.

a. WHAT ARE SHARES?

Shares indicate ownership of a corporation. If a corporation issues 100,000 shares and if you buy 1,000 of these, you own 1% of the company.

Corporations issue shares to raise money. Let us assume that you have a great idea for manufacturing widgets that will generate large profits. But you need start-up capital of $1 million. So you start a corporation and issue 200,000 shares at $10 each. You keep 100,000 shares or 50% of the company for yourself and sell the remaining 100,000 shares at $10 each. This gives you the $1 million you need to manufacture widgets.

Once these shares are issued, investors who bought these shares will not normally be able to sell them back to the corporation. But they can sell them to other investors. The price of these shares on any given day is determined by market forces — supply and demand. If there are more buyers than sellers, the price will go up; if there are more sellers than buyers, the price will come down. If the corporation makes large profits, the price of the shares will go up. If it makes large losses, the price will come down.

Within a single day the price may go up or down several times, depending on supply and demand for that stock on that day.

b. HOW ARE SHARES TRADED?

Generally, stocks are bought and sold from a few central locations called stock exchanges (such as the New York Stock Exchange and the Toronto Stock Exchange). Shares are traded at the exchanges through auction.

c. HOW TO BUY AND SELL SHARES

If you want to buy or sell shares, you need to go through a stockbroker who will arrange for the transaction to take place. The normal procedure is to simply call your broker on the telephone and place an order to buy or sell a certain number of shares of a stock.

d. HOW TO FIND A STOCKBROKER

There are two kinds of stockbrokers: full service and discount. *Full service brokers* charge a higher commission, but they are likely to provide the information you need about your stock. They also make recommendations regarding what stock to buy. A good full service stockbroker will try to understand your objectives, how much risk you want to take with your money, and whether a given investment is suitable for you or not. *Discount brokers,* on the other hand, simply take your order and execute it. Because they don't provide any additional service, their commission charges are lower.

Many people choose brokers by "word of mouth" — on the recommendation of friends and acquaintances. The other way to choose a broker is to look through the Yellow Pages and pick a firm that is a member in all major exchanges. Call the firm and ask to talk to a broker. You will be put in touch with the "broker of the day." He or she will probably arrange to have a personal meeting with you and take down all the required information to open an account. Once the account is opened, you can carry out all the transactions over the telephone.

e. HOW TO PLACE ORDERS WITH YOUR BROKER

Once you decide what stock to buy, you can simply call your broker to buy "100 shares of XYZ company at $ ___ per share." If you do not specify a price that you are willing to pay, your broker will buy shares *at the market price* (the price at which the stock is available when your order reaches the stock exchange).

If you specify a price at which the stock should be bought, you have placed what is known as a Good Till Canceled (GTC) order. A GTC order will remain with the broker until the order is executed or you cancel the order. Suppose XYZ stock is trading at $10.25 and you do not want to pay more than $10 for it. You may place an order to buy 100 shares of XYZ at $10. Your order will be active for about 30 days. During this time, if XYZ sells for $10, it will be bought at that price for you.

f. WHAT ELSE SHOULD YOU KNOW?

Stocks are usually sold in multiples of 100. One hundred shares are called a *board lot* or a *round lot*. You can of course buy less than 100 shares. When you buy less than 100 shares, you are said to be dealing in *odd lots*. However, commission charges are higher for odd lots.

The price of a stock *usually* goes up or down by a minimum of one-eighth of a dollar (e.g., 7⅛, 7¼, 7⅜). Lower-priced stocks go up and down in steps of 1/16 or 1/32 of a dollar. Penny stocks (very low-priced stocks) go up or down in steps of one cent.

g. WHAT ARE OTC STOCKS?

Some stocks are not traded through stock exchanges. Instead, they are traded through an electronic network of dealers. The stocks traded this way are called over-the-counter (OTC) stocks. While there may be exciting opportunities in this sector of the market, you should be aware of certain disadvantages:

- Less information is readily available about OTC stocks.

- You may find that few newspapers carry complete listings of these stocks. Every time you want to know the price at which these stocks are trading, you have to call your broker.

h. HOW TO READ THE FINANCIAL PAGE

Each day, major newspapers list the stocks that are traded in the main stock exchanges. They are usually listed as follows:

12-Month				PE				
High	Low	Stock	Volume	Ratio	High	Low	Close	Change
16	12	NSF Bank	20,000	20	15	13	14½	-½

The third column (Stock) indicates the name of the company whose stocks are under consideration. The first two columns (12-Month High/Low) indicates that in the past 12 months, NSF Bank shares were sold as high as $16 a share, and as low as $12 a share. The Volume column indicates how many shares changed hands during the day. PE ratio (price earnings ratio) is explained in section j. below. In general, the lower the PE ratio, the better it is from an investment point of view.

The next three columns summarize the previous day's transactions: the stock sold for as high as $15 and as low as $13, and the last trade occurred at $14½. The last column shows the difference between yesterday's closing and the previous day's closing. In the example, yesterday's closing price was $14½. The change is $½, that is, the previous day's closing price was $15.

i. WHAT IS A STOP-LOSS ORDER?

Suppose you buy a stock at $10, hoping that it will increase in value. Since you can never be certain of this, you may want to limit your losses should the price fall. You may decide to take a loss of 15%, but not much more. In this case, you may enter a stop-loss order with your broker at $8.50. If the price of the stock reaches $8.50, your broker will automatically sell your shares at the best possible price available at that time.

j. HOW TO MINIMIZE THE RISK

The stock you buy can either go up or go down. Although we all hope that the stocks we buy will go up, there is no guarantee. To minimize the risk of losing money on a stock, you may want to follow these guidelines.

1. Buy stocks with low price earnings (PE) ratio

Suppose a share costs $10 and the company earns $2 per share. That is, the company makes $2 for each $10 you invest. The price earnings is simply

$$\text{PE ratio} = \frac{\text{Price per share}}{\text{Earnings per share}} = \frac{\$10}{\$2} = 5$$

The higher the earnings, the lower the PE ratio. Therefore, if the PE ratio is low, say six or lower, the price of the stock is less likely to go down compared to another stock with a much higher PE ratio (all things being equal). Financial pages report the PE ratios of most major stocks daily.

2. Buy stocks with high book values

Book value tells us how much a company is worth. For example, if a company had net assets of $100 million with 10 million shares outstanding, its book value is $100 million divided by 10 million = $10 per share.

If the company ceased to operate, each share would still be worth $10. Therefore, it is safer to buy stocks that trade close to and lower than their book value. Book values are not usually reported in the financial pages of the newspapers. Perhaps the simplest way to find out the book value of any given stock is to ask your broker.

k. COMMISSIONS: HOW TO REDUCE THEM

Whenever you buy or sell shares, you have to pay a commission to the broker. This could be as high as 3% when you buy, and 3% when you sell. Many brokerage houses have a minimum commission of $40 to $60. In return for this commission, a full-service brokerage house will provide research information and advice on stocks.

However, many small investors may find the commission costs rather high. If you are sure of what you want to buy, then you can save on commissions by going to discount brokerage houses. Discount brokerage houses generally will not offer you any advice. They will simply execute your orders.

If you want to use a discount broker, make sure that the discounts offered are meaningful. If you write to them, they will send you a schedule of their charges for different transactions. You can then compare and decide.

Many discount brokers advertise their services in newspapers such as the *Wall Street Journal* and the *New York Times* (for the United States), or the *Globe and Mail Report on Business* (for Canada).

Here is a partial list of some discount brokers in the United States and Canada. (For a full list with names, addresses, and phone numbers, see the Resources Directory at the end of this book.)

United States

- Accutrade

- American Express Financial Direct
- Andrew Peck Associates
- Arnold Securities
- Aufhauser & Company
- Bidwell & Company
- Bull & Bear Securities
- Ceres Securities
- Charles Schwab
- CompuTEL Securities
- Datek Securities
- ebroker
- E*Trade
- Fidelity Investments
- Freedom Investments
- Icahn & Company
- Jack White & Company
- J.B. Oxford & Company
- Marquette DeBary Company
- National Discount Brokers
- Net Investor
- Pacific Brokerage Services
- Pacific Continental Securities
- PC Financial Networth
- Quick and Reilly
- Regal Discount Securities
- Savoy Discount Brokerage
- Scottsdale Securities

- T. Rowe Price Discount Brokerage
- USAA Brokerage Services
- Wall Street Access
- The Wall Street Discount Corporation
- Waterhouse Securities
- White Discount Securities

Canada

- Affinity Investments
- Bank of Montreal Investor Services
- CIBC Investors Edge
- CT Market Partner
- Hongkong Bank Discount Trading
- Royal Bank Action Direct
- Scotia Discount Brokerage
- Toronto-Dominion Green Line

1. WHY DIRECT INVESTMENT MAY NOT BE SUITABLE FOR THE SMALL INVESTOR

Although I have discussed stock market investments at considerable length, direct stock market investments may not be suitable for the small investor for the following reasons:

(a) *Individual stocks can be expensive.* For example, in fall of 1998, Microsoft shares were selling at $120 per share. To buy 100 shares, an investor would need as much as $12,000.

(b) *The commission can be high.* For example, for the above transaction you may have to pay more than $360 in commission charges. When you sell you may have to pay another $360.

(c) *You cannot spread the risk.* Even after spending $11,280, you hold only one stock, you are totally dependent on this company thriving for you to make money.

Obviously, it would be preferable for the small investor to find a stock market investment medium that is less expensive, involves little commission, and is less risky.

Is there such a medium?

Yes, there is! In fact, you can start with as low as $100, pay no commission, and spread the risk.

m. HOW YOU CAN PARTICIPATE IN THE STOCK MARKET

The investment medium I am talking about is *mutual funds.* As mentioned earlier, a mutual fund is an investment company whose main purpose is the investment and management of investors' money. When you invest your money in a mutual fund, it is pooled with that of other investors and is invested in a wide variety of stocks. This minimizes your cost as well as your risk.

Some mutual funds charge a commission; others do not. Those that do not charge a commission are called *no-load mutual funds.* There is no evidence to show that funds that charge a commission perform better than those that do not. Hence, a new investor is better off investing in a no-load fund.

No-load mutual funds have the following advantages:

- *No sales commissions.*

- *No high-pressure salespeople.* No-load funds have no salespeople; that's the reason you do not pay any commission.

51

- *Greater safety.* Since the fund invests in a variety of companies, the investment is diversified. This usually minimizes your risk.

- *Ease of operation.* Obviously it is easier to buy and sell a single fund than a wide variety of stocks. Some funds allow you to buy and sell over the telephone.

- *Variety.* There are several types of funds. These include funds that specialize in high-dividend-yielding stocks (income funds); funds that invest in stocks that are likely to appreciate greatly in value (growth stocks); funds that invest in stocks that relate to natural resources; funds that invest in foreign securities (international funds); and funds that invest in bonds (bond funds). Depending on your requirements, you can choose a fund that is right for you.

Given all these advantages, the no-load mutual fund is perhaps the best way for a beginner to get started in the stock market.

For further information on selecting a mutual fund, you can obtain The Investment Company Institute's *Directory of Mutual Funds.* The 1998 edition of this guide contains information on over 7,000 U.S. mutual funds.

The Investment Company Institute
1401 H Street N.W.
Washington, DC 20005
Phone: (202) 326-5800
www.ici.org

For an extensive list of no-load or low-load mutual funds (including the minimum required and the nature of each fund), you may want to consult *Individual Investor's Guide to Low-Load Mutual Funds.* It is published by the American Association of Individual Investors and costs $24.95 (It is free with membership in the organization). The guide has detailed information on over 900 funds, including their performances, share data, portfolio, and shareholder information.

If you are a small investor, the following no-load mutual funds may be suitable for you since the minimum amount to join is $200 or less.

United States

- Capstone Growth

- Dupree KY Tax-Free Income

- Dupree KY Tax-Free Short-to-Medium

(The addresses and phone numbers for the above funds are in the Resource Directory.)

Canada

No-load equity funds are very popular in Canada. Consequently there are many more no-load mutual funds today than there were about ten years ago. Most funds, however, require a minimum — usually between $100 and $1,000. Here are some funds that require no amount to join and are RRSP eligible in Canada:

- CCS Fonds Action

- Empire Equity Growth

- Ind Alliance Cdn. Adv N

- Ind Alliance Stock ANL

- Ind Alliance Stocks

- Ind Alliance Stock Ser 2

- National Trust Cdn. Index

- PH&N Vintage Fund

- Transamerica Agent Plan

If you need additional information, contact:

The Investment Fund Institute of Canada
151 Yonge Street, 5th Floor
Toronto, ON M5C 2W7
Phone: (416) 363-2158
www.mutfunds.com/ific/

Ask for the institute's membership list. The list gives the addresses and phone numbers of several mutual funds. Examine the performance of these funds with other funds as well. Performance of all Canadian funds are published monthly by the *National Post* and the *Globe and Mail Report on Business.* (The *Globe and Mail* and the *National Post* compare the performance of several Canadian funds on ten-year, five-year, three-year, one-year, and quarterly and monthly bases. This survey is usually published in the third week of every month). Contact those funds that have performed well over the years to find out their terms and conditions.

n. HOW TO CHOOSE A FUND

Choosing a fund among the several that are available depends on several factors.

(a) *The amount of money you have.* Different funds have different minimum investment requirements. You are obviously restricted by the amount of money you have to invest.

(b) *Your investment needs.* As mentioned earlier, different funds are geared to different needs. For example, if you want high current yield, an income fund is a better choice. If you are not interested in high current income but would rather invest in stocks that are likely to increase substantially in value, you would choose a growth fund. Or you may prefer to invest in different types of funds as money becomes available to you.

(c) *Funds' past performance.* A fund that has done consistently well in the past is likely to do well in the future. The performance of a fund should be judged over a period of time (at least the five previous years) and not just on the past 12 months. Any fund can do well or badly in a given year. Consistently good performance, on the other hand, seldom happens by chance.

To give you sufficient flexibility, I have listed a wide variety of funds in the United States and Canada in the Resource Directory at the end of this book. Before subscribing to any of the funds, obtain prospectuses from different funds and compare their differences and long-term performances.

7

HOW TO BUY STOCKS AT A DISCOUNT

When you go to a discount broker, you pay a lower commission. But there is a way to avoid commissions completely. In fact, you can even buy stocks at a discount! This may sound too good to be true, but you can do it by taking advantage of a less-widely known program called DRIP.

a. DIVIDEND REINVESTMENT INVESTMENT PLANS (DRIPs)

DRIPs stands for "Dividend Reinvestment Investment Plans." As you know, many stocks pay regular dividends. Some stocks that pay regular dividends have set up DRIPs that let you reinvest your dividends without commissions.

All you have to do to join the DRIP program of a given stock is own just one share in the company. Once you buy the share, you should register the stock in your name. The transfer agent for the company will send you the necessary forms. Indicate that you want to be in the DRIP program. You will then receive all the necessary details.

b. THE ADVANTAGES OF JOINING A DRIP

DRIPs offer you an opportunity to reinvest the dividends you receive in additional stocks automatically. In most cases, no commission is involved. Many companies will let you buy additional shares, and others will let you buy shares at a 5% discount.

If you add this 5% discount to the 2% commission that you would normally pay, you see that you pay $100 for what would cost most people $107. A 7% return on your investment before you even start is not a bad deal!

Dividend-paying companies tend to be established, stable companies. Therefore, you have a degree of safety built in when you join the DRIP program offered by a company.

Here are the advantages of joining a DRIP program:

- Your dividends are automatically reinvested.

- You may be allowed to buy more shares with no commission.

- In some cases, you may buy shares at a discount.

- Your investment is relatively safe.

c. INFORMATION ON DRIP COMPANIES

You can obtain information on companies that participate in the DRIP program from stock exchanges.

United States

In the United States, there are also newsletters that specialize in DRIP investing. An example of such a newsletter is:

DRIP Investor
7412 Calumet Avenue
Hammond, IN 46324-2692
www.dripinvestor.com

DRIP Investor also offers a Directory of Dividend Reinvestment Plans at no charge (call 1-800-233-5922).

Canada

In Canada, the Toronto Stock Exchange, for example, provides a listing of DRIP companies along with their terms and conditions. This can be purchased for about $15. (For the addresses of the Toronto and other stock exchanges, see the Resource Directory at the end of the book.) If you are interested in DRIPs, you should contact stock exchanges for more details.

d. HOW TO JOIN A DRIP

If you are interested in a DRIP program, this is what you should do:

(a) Get a list of companies that offer a DRIP program by contacting the stock exchanges.

(b) Go through the list and choose those companies that seem attractive to you.

(c) Of these companies, see which ones have more favorable terms.

(d) Buy some stocks in each company you are interested in by going through a stockbroker. (There also other methods: you can buy DRIP stock in some financial trade shows or through some organizations. These methods are beyond the scope of this book.)

(e) Get the forms from the "transfer agent" for the company.

(f) Fill out the form indicating that you would like to be in the DRIP program.

(g) Once you have done this, you will automatically receive information which will enable you take advantage of the DRIP program.

e. WHAT ELSE SHOULD YOU KNOW?

While DRIP investing is attractive, please bear in mind that only a handful of companies offer this program. Many companies that are attractive from an investment point of view may not offer a DRIP program. You should definitely consider a DRIP program, but you should also consider that avoiding commissions and buying a stock at a discount is only one aspect of investing. The real meat of investing is in making your money grow. If you find a stock that makes your money grow faster, don't let go of the opportunity just because it does not offer a DRIP program.

8

HOW TO INVEST IN BONDS

a. WHAT ARE BONDS?

Governments and corporations need to borrow money from time to time. To do this, they issue bonds to the public. Thus, when you buy a bond, you are lending your money to the government or to the corporation for a specified period of time. In return for this, you are paid regular interest.

Every bond has three features:

(a) A *face value* or the loan amount (usually $1,000)

(b) A specified *rate of interest* (called the *coupon* rate)

(c) A *maturity date* (the date on which the company or government will buy the bond back from you at the face value)

Suppose you buy a bond that matures after ten years. What happens if you need the money after five years? The company or the government will not normally buy it back from you until the maturity (or redemption) date. However, you can sell it to some other investor in the bond market. When you sell your bond to another investor in the open market, the price you get will depend on supply and demand factors. You may get less than what you paid for it or you may get more.

b. BOND PRICES

What determines how much you will get for your bond before the maturity date? It depends on interest rates. If interest rates are higher when you want to sell than when you bought the bonds, you will get a lower price for your bonds. If the interest rates are lower when you want to sell than when you bought the bonds, you will get a higher price for your bonds. In short, when interest rates go up, the prices come down; when the interest rates come down, the prices go up.

Suppose you buy a bond for $1,000 and the interest rate is 10%. If the interest rate paid by financial institutions such as banks moves up to 12%, then investors will not be willing to pay $1,000 for your bond, because your bond pays only 10% interest and they can get 12% buying newly issued bonds. But if you sell your bond at a discount, say for $850, investors will buy it from you. When this happens, your bond is said to be *trading at a discount*. Although you sold your bond at $850, when the maturity date arrives, the person holding the bond will get the full $1,000. The difference between what you got ($1,000) and what you paid ($850) is known as "capital gains." Capital gains are taxed at a low rate in the United States and in Canada.

On the other hand, suppose you buy a bond for $1,000 and the interest rate is 10%. If the interest rate moves down to 8%, then investors may be willing to pay more than $1,000 for your bond, because new bonds pay only 8% interest while yours pays 10%. You may be able to sell your bond, for example, for $1,150. When this happens, your bond is said to be *trading at a premium*. Although you sold your bond at $1,150, when the maturity date arrives, the person holding the bond will get only $1,000.

c. WHEN TO BUY BONDS

Because the value of bonds goes up when the interest rate goes down, *you should buy bonds when you expect the interest rate to go down*. When the price of the bond you bought goes up and you sell, you make a profit and this profit will be treated as capital gains. Capital gains usually get good tax treatment in the United States and Canada. You should be careful when buying a bond that trades at a premium. Unless the interest rate comes down before the maturity date, you will get back less than the amount you paid for it.

d. BONDS AND DEBENTURES

Bonds are generally issued with collateral. The company issuing a bond backs it up with specific assets. Debentures, on the other hand, are issued without any collateral. You buy debentures based on the reputation of the company issuing it. All government "bonds" are really debentures — you cannot force the government to sell off the parliament building to repay your bond. How do you know how safe your bond is? There are independent bond rating services that rate all bonds. Your broker should be able to tell you the rating of any major bond. Safer bonds tend to have slightly lower interest rates compared to bonds that are less safe.

e. HOW TO BUY

Bonds can be bought and sold through a stockbroker. The commission costs for bonds are much lower than for stocks.

f. BOND AND MORTGAGE FUNDS

Since most bonds cost around $1,000, a small investor may not be able to diversify properly with bonds. Besides, many investors may not want to be bothered about selecting suitable bonds for their portfolios. *Bond funds* overcome these problems by pooling the money received from many investors and investing it in a portfolio of bonds, mortgages, or both. Interest rates influence bond funds in the same way that interest rates influence bonds.

The following U.S. bond funds require a minimum of $500 to join (for addresses and phone numbers see the Resource Directory at the back of the book):

61

- Aquinas Fixed Income
- Babson Bond Trust — Port L
- Babson Bond Trust — Port S
- Excelsior Interm-Term Managed Income
- Excelsior Managed Income
- Homestead Short-Term Bond

The following Canadian bond funds require $50 or less to join (for addresses and phone numbers see the Resource Directory):

- Barreau Quebec Bond (No minimum)
- CDA Fixed Income (No minimum)
- CSS Fonds Obligataire (No minimum)
- GWL Bond (B) NL ($50 minimum)
- GWL Bond (S) NL ($50 minimum)
- GWL Cdn. Bond (G) NL ($50 minimum)
- GWL Global Income (A) NL ($50 minimum)
- GWL Govt. Bond (G) NL ($50 minimum)
- GWL Income (M) NL ($50 minimum)
- GWL Intl. Bond (P) NL ($50 minimum)
- Ind Alliance Bond BNL (No minimum)
- Ind Alliance Bonds S-2 (No minimum)
- Ind Alliance Cdn. Bond (No minimum)
- Ind Alliance Global Bond (No minimum)
- Ind Alliance Income R (No minimum)
- Westbury Cdn. Life Bond ($30 minimum)

There are over 275 bond and mortgage funds in Canada. There are even more in the United States. See the Resource Directory for a listing of some of these funds.

g. STRIPS AND ZEROS

Stripped bonds are like any other bearer bond in that they are issued with coupons attached to them so bond holders can exchange the "coupons" for interest payments. To "strip" a bond, an investment dealer buys a block of these bonds and removes all the coupons. The bond is then called the "residue." You can buy either the "coupon" part or the "residue" part. If you buy the coupon part, you get the regular interest rate, but you will not benefit if the price of the bond goes up.

If you buy the residue part, you will get no interest at all, but you will pay a much lower price to buy the bond. For instance, if you can find a stripped bond that matures in 25 years with a 12% coupon, you need to invest only $5,825 today to receive $100,000 at the end of the term. Stripped bonds also rise sharply when the interest rate goes down.

Zero coupon bonds are similar to stripped bonds in that you can buy a $1,000 bond for a fraction of its face value. You will not be paid any interest, but when the bond matures you will be able to redeem it for its full face value.

The main attraction of these bonds is that they enable you to lock in at a high yield for a long time. This is particularly advantageous if interest rates go down in the future. On the other hand, if interest rates go up, you will be locked into a lower yield. If you want to sell your bond at that time, you will get a much lower price than you paid for it. Even small fluctuations in interest rates will make the market price of these bonds go up and down.

One main disadvantage of these strips in Canada is that you are expected to pay taxes regularly even though you do not receive any interest. The interest is deemed to have been received by you on a regular basis for tax purposes. (Canadian investors may buy stripped bonds for their Registered Retirement Savings Plans [RRSPs] where it is not taxed until the plan is closed.)

You can use strips and zeros to your advantage by buying a few bonds each year with different maturity dates. These may be used to supplement your income in later years.

There are also mutual funds that invest in zero coupon bonds. (These funds are U.S.–based.) You may want to consider the following zero coupon funds:

- Benham Target Maturities Trust series 2000

- Benham Target Maturities Trust series 2005

- Benham Target Maturities Trust series 2010

- Benham Target Maturities Trust series 2015

- Benham Target Maturities Trust series 2020

All these funds are no-load and require a minimum investment of $1,000. To get the prospectus for any or all of these funds, please contact:

Benham Management Corp.
1665 Charleston Road
Mountain View, CA 94043
Phone: 1-800-321-8321 / (415) 965-4222

h. CONVERTIBLE BONDS

Convertible bonds are like any other bond except for one special feature: they give you the privilege of exchanging the bonds for a specified number of shares of the company before a certain date. Because of this attractive feature, the interest rate is usually lower.

For example, Rogers Communications has a convertible bond which pays a fixed interest rate of 7.5%. You can also exchange this bond for 4.83 shares of Rogers Communications. Rogers Communications was trading at $10 (in mid-October, 1998). Suppose the price of these shares moves up to $15. Since you can convert your bond into 4.83 shares, it will now be worth at least $72.45 (4.83 x $15). In fact it will be worth more because the bond pays interest as well. Thus, when share prices rise, convertible bonds automatically benefit.

On the other hand, suppose the stock goes down to $5 per share. Then the share value of your bond will be only $24.15 (4.83 x $5). But the price of the bond will not decline that much because, unlike the shares, convertible bonds pay interest. Thus, when share prices decline, convertible bonds will not decline to the same extent.

In other words, when the share prices increase, convertible bonds behave like shares with unlimited profit potential. When share prices go down, convertible bonds are partially protected against corresponding declines because of their interest yielding feature.

1. What to look for in convertible bonds

The convertible feature is of no great benefit if the total value of the share per bond is too low relative to the cost of the bond. This would mean that the shares have to move up significantly before you can make a profit. Therefore, when you buy a convertible bond, you should make sure that the premium is not too high. (Higher premiums will be asked for when the underlying stock is expected to move up and when the bond has a high coupon.) Premium is calculated as follows:

$$\text{Percent premium} = \frac{(100 \times \text{Current bond price})}{(\text{No. of shares per bond} \times \text{Current stock price})} - 100$$

You also have to look for the actual rate of interest. This is calculated as follows:

$$\text{Percent current interest} = \frac{(100 \times \text{Interest specified on the bond})}{\text{Current bond price}}$$

You should look for convertible bonds with low premiums and high current yield. Bonds trading close to (or below) their par value are more desirable than bonds that trade at a price that is much higher.

2. When to buy convertible bonds

A convertible bond is a good buy when —

- the current interest on the bond is not too low compared to regular bonds,
- the conversion is relatively low (under 20%),
- there are reasons to believe that the underlying stock will rise,
- interest rates are falling, but the stock is rising, and
- the bond is not trading above its par value (usually $1,000).

The last feature is particularly important because many convertible bonds have a "call feature" which gives the corporation the right to buy the bond back at a specified price on or after a specified date. Once a bond is called, you will get only the specified price, no matter how much you paid to get it.

You have to be careful when —

- the bond is selling much above its face value,
- the conversion premium is high but the current yield is low,
- the call features are due soon,
- the interest rates are rising but the share prices are falling,
- the share price is not likely to go up, and/or
- the underlying company is not sound.

There are hardly any convertible bond funds in Canada. Even in the United States there are only a few. These funds either charge a commission or have lackluster performance, or both.

Convertible bonds can be very profitable, provided you choose the right ones at the right time. You might be better off investing directly in them (if you find good convertible bonds) rather than through a mutual fund.

3. How is the gain taxed?

The interest paid on the bond is fully taxed as interest income. If the bond goes up in price and you sell it, the profit will be treated as capital gains and taxed (or not taxed) accordingly.

9

HOW TO INVEST IN PREFERRED STOCKS

a. WHAT IS A PREFERRED STOCK?

A preferred stock, like a common stock, represents shares of ownership in a company. A preferred stock carries a fixed rate of dividend. This dividend must be paid before any dividend on common stocks. However, preferred shares do not carry voting rights.

Although a preferred stock technically represents ownership, it works like a bond. There are some differences:

- Bonds pay an indicated rate of interest while preferred stocks pay an indicated rate of dividend.

- In general, the interest you receive from bonds is fully taxed (there are some exceptions to this rule), while dividends received on preferred stocks will be taxed at a favorable rate.

- Bonds in general have a maturity date, the day on which you will receive the face value of the bond; preferred shares do not have maturity dates.

- Most bonds have a face value of $1,000. Interest is calculated on this face value, no matter what price you paid to buy the bond. Most preferred shares have a face value of $25.

b. WHY INVEST IN A PREFERRED STOCK?

In spite of their differences, both bonds and preferred shares are bought for steady income. Preferred stocks are bought for exactly the same reasons as bonds. Whether you buy bonds or preferred stocks depends on your tax situation and the level of security you want with your income.

c. DIFFERENT KINDS OF PREFERRED STOCKS

Some corporations issue Class A preferred shares, Class B preferred shares, and so on. In such cases, Class A share dividends must be paid before Class B share dividends, Class B before Class C, and so on. Class A preferred shares would then be called *prior preferred*.

Certain types of preferred shares are known as *participating preferreds*. Holders of these preferreds are entitled to additional dividends if the common stock dividends exceed a certain amount.

Cumulative preferreds guarantee that the accumulated dividend will be paid later if it cannot be paid when it is due. Such payments will take precedence over common stock dividends.

Convertible preferreds are similar to convertible bonds in that they can be exchanged for a specified number of common shares at the holder's option. This feature is attractive if the common stock is on its way up.

Retractable preferreds give the holder the right to redeem his or her shares after a specific date at a specific price. This feature may be useful should the value of the preferred stock decline.

Except in the case of convertible preferreds, preferred shares are generally bought for high current yields. Preferred shares do not have the same potential for appreciation, except when interest rates are on the decline. Newer issues, however, have some innovative features (like variable interest rates) that make them attractive as a conservative investment medium. You should look into these features before you invest.

d. PREFERRED STOCK PRICES

Once issued to the public, preferred stock trades on stock exchanges. The price of a preferred stock will depend on prevailing interest rates. If the interest rates are higher when you want to sell than when you bought the preferred stock, you will get a lower price than what you paid. If the interest rates are lower when you want to sell than when you bought the preferred stock, you will get a higher price for your preferred stock. In short, when the interest rates go up, the prices come down; when the interest rates come down, the prices go up. Preferred share prices go up and down with interest rates, but in the opposite direction. This is exactly how bonds behave as well.

e. WHEN TO BUY PREFERRED STOCKS

Because the value of preferred stocks goes up when the interest rate goes down, you should buy preferred stocks when you expect the interest rate to go down. When the price of the preferred stock you bought goes up and you sell, you make a profit and this profit will be treated as capital gains. Capital gains usually get better tax treatment in the United States and Canada.

f. HOW TO BUY AND SELL PREFERRED STOCKS

Because preferred shares trade on stock exchanges, you would buy preferred shares in the same way you would buy bonds: through your stockbroker.

g. USING MUTUAL FUNDS TO BUY PREFERRED STOCKS

There are mutual funds that specialize in dividend income. Most of these mutual funds are heavily invested in preferred stocks. (They also invest in dividend-paying common stocks.) Here are some no-load, dividend-income mutual funds:

United States

In the United States, mutual funds are not generally identified as preferred income funds. If you are interested in dividend oriented stocks, you should look for "Growth and Income Funds." I recommend that you consult *Low-Load Mutual Funds*, published each year by the American Association of Individual Investors.

Canada

- Canada Trust Dividend Inc. ($500 minimum)
- CIBC Dividend ($500 minimum)
- First Cdn. Dividend Income ($500 minimum)
- GWL Div/Gro (M) NL ($50 minimum)
- GWL Dividend (G) NL ($50 minimum)
- Hongkong Bank Div Income ($500 minimum)
- Ind Alliance Dividend V (No minimum)
- InvesNat Dividend ($500 minimum)
- IRIS Dividend Fund ($500 minimum)
- Millennia Cdn. Div Ser 2 ($500 minimum)
- Mutual Summit Div Growth ($500 minimum)
- National Trust Dividend ($500 minimum)
- Scotia Excel Dividend ($500 minimum)

10

HOW TO INVEST INTERNATIONALLY

a. WHY INVEST ABROAD?

Many investors think that only the rich should invest in foreign countries. But there is money to be made in foreign countries, and foreign investing is not difficult. You do not need a lot of money either.

In the one-year period ending October 1998, the U.S. stock market gained 7.9% and the Canadian stock market fell 4.4%. For the same period, the Belgian stock market gained 42.1%, the French stock market 32.2%, the German stock market 26.3%, the Italian stock market 59.8%, the Spanish stock market 46.8%, and the Swiss stock market 33.9%.

Why shouldn't you have a piece of the action? Different countries grow at different rates. By investing only in Canada or in the United States, you can miss the growth that is taking place elsewhere. The world is becoming smaller and smaller. If you arbitrarily decide to invest only in North America, it is unlikely that you will do as well as you would if you invested abroad. If you had started with about $500 in 1960 and shifted the money into different markets at the right time, you would have well over $1 million by now! (See Chart #2.) Yet you would have moved your money only 16 times in 25 years!

Since the chart was produced about five years ago, you could have increased your investment by another 50% (another $500,000) by simply moving your investments three more times!

CHART #2
INTERNATIONAL INVESTMENTS
Turning $500 into $1,000,000

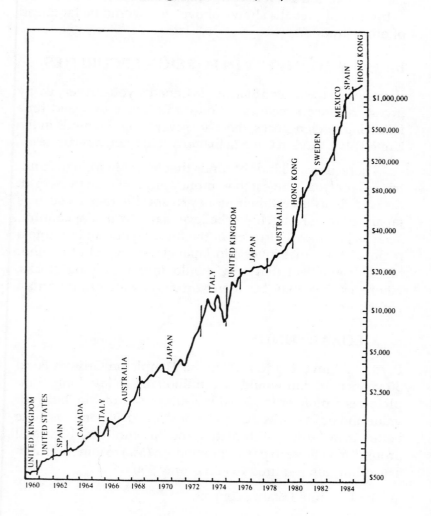

Concept and data: International Bank Credit Analyst and Capital International Perspective (brought to the author's attention by Adrian Day).

I am not suggesting that you could have predicted precisely which country would do well. I don't think anybody can do that. But even if you could achieve a fraction of the extraordinary results shown above, you would be far ahead of other investors.

b. HOW TO INVEST IN FOREIGN SECURITIES

If you live in the United States or in Canada, you can very easily invest in foreign securities. You do not have to spend time following foreign stocks; there are several mutual funds in the United States and in Canada that invest in foreign securities.

There are two kinds of funds that invest in foreign countries. *Global funds* invest their money anywhere in the world. *Regional funds* invest their money in specific regions such as Japan or Hong Kong. If you believe that a particular country, such as Japan, will do well in the future, you can buy into a regional fund that invests in Japanese stocks. On the other hand, if you feel that you should invest in good stocks, wherever they may be, then you may want to buy into a global fund.

c. GLOBAL FUNDS

If you had invested $30,000 in the Templeton Growth Fund 30 years ago, you would be a millionaire today. John Templeton is a pioneer in global investing. Templeton looks for value and buys stocks that are undervalued. No one has done better than he has. Templeton and his fund are both still around. You have to pay a commission (6%) to join this fund. The minimum required to join is only $500.

In the United States, contact:

Templeton Growth Fund
700 Central Avenue
Box 33030
St. Petersburg, FL 33701
Phone: 1-800-237-0738 / (813) 823-8712

In Canada, contact:

Templeton Growth Fund
4 W. King Street, 19th Floor
Toronto, ON M5W 1N3
Phone: 1-800-387-0830 / (416) 364-4672

There are many mutual funds that invest internationally. Here are some funds that charge no commissions, have low minimums, and have higher one-year returns. Their addresses and phone numbers can be found in the Resource Directory at the end of the book.

United States

- Columbia Intl. Stock
- Excelsior International
- Excelsior Pan European
- Gabelli Global Telecommunications
- INVESCO Worldwide Communications
- Montgomery Global Communications
- Montgomery Select 50-R
- Neuberger & Berman International
- Scout Worldwide

Canada

- Altamira European Equity
- CDA European
- First Canadian European Growth
- Green Line European Growth
- Hongkong Bank European Growth
- InvesNat European Equity
- Montrusco Select UK Equity

- Royal European Growth
- Scudder Greater European

d. REGIONAL FUNDS

If you are interested in investing in a specific country, you can do so through a closed-end fund. A closed-end fund is a company whose sole business is to invest its capital for its shareholders. Once a closed-end fund starts operating, it will not accept new money from investors. But you can buy and sell shares in a closed-end fund just like you would buy and sell the shares of any publicly traded company — on a stock exchange. Some of these funds can trade at a premium or at a discount from their net asset value. If you want to invest in any of these funds, you may want to ask your broker whether the fund is trading at a discount or at a premium. You should avoid funds that are trading at a premium, especially if the premium is large. Here are a few funds that invest in different countries:

- Asia Pacific Fund (New York Stock Exchange)
- Emerging Mexico Fund (New York Stock Exchange)
- Europe Investment Concept Fund (New York Stock Exchange)
- First Asia Income Fund (Toronto Stock Exchange)
- First Israel Fund (New York Stock Exchange)
- First Philippine Fund (New York Stock Exchange)
- Growth of Spain Fund (New York Stock Exchange)
- India Fund (New York Stock Exchange)
- Indonesia Fund (New York Stock Exchange)
- Italy Fund (New York Stock Exchange)
- Japan Equity Fund (New York Stock Exchange)
- Korea Fund (New York Stock Exchange)

- Malaysia Fund (New York Stock Exchange)
- New Germany Fund (Toronto Stock Exchange)
- Swiss Helvetica Fund (New York Stock Exchange)
- Taiwan Fund (New York Stock Exchange)
- Thai Capital Fund (New York Stock Exchange)
- United Kingdom Fund (New York Stock Exchange)

e. BEFORE YOU START

If you want to invest in foreign securities, I suggest that you write to different funds and compare their track records before investing. You may also want to read a good book on international investing. There are several books on the market. Buy a recent one. The market is changing fast.

11
HOW TO INVEST IN GOLD

a. WHY INVEST IN GOLD?

If you keep your money in the bank, you earn interest on your savings. If you buy stocks, you may be paid dividends. If you invest in a business, you may get a share of profits. Gold, on the other hand, does not provide any return on a regular basis on your investment.

Why, then, are we talking about gold as an investment? Why should small investors even bother to consider gold as part of an investment program?

To understand the importance of gold as a form of investment, you need to understand the price history of gold:

Year	Average price per oz.	% Increase
1968	$39	—
1973	98	151%
1978	193	395
1982	376	865
1987	447	1046
1994	381	877
1998	290	650

People buy gold for capital gains! They expect the gold price to move up with inflation over long periods.

Until about ten years ago, gold kept pace with inflation. In recent years, however, because of low inflation and a very strong U.S. dollar, gold has lost its luster. However, many investors still believe that gold provides ultimate stability during unstable times. As such it always has the potential to go up in price unexpectedly, and within a short period. For this reason many sophisticated investors hold some gold.

One caution — don't forget that gold prices are volatile. This means the price of gold could go down in the short run and stay at that level for quite some time. A small investor must make sure not to invest any money in gold that might be needed in an emergency.

b. SOME COMMON WAYS TO PARTICIPATE IN THE GOLD MARKET

There are several ways in which an investor can participate in the gold market. Not all methods are suitable for the small investor. I will first discuss some of the common methods used, and then identify those that are suitable for the small investor.

There are five ways in which an investor can participate in the gold market. These are:

(a) Gold bullion (gold bars)

(b) Gold coins

(c) Gold certificates

(d) Gold stocks

(e) Gold futures

1. Gold bullion

Gold bullion is simply a gold bar. Gold bars are produced in a wide variety of sizes, ranging from 5 grams to 400 ounces. The gold prices quoted in the newspapers refer to the price per ounce for a standard 400-ounce gold bar. If you buy smaller bars, costs will be higher, since a bar charge is added to the standard price quoted. Bar charges can be in excess of 10% of the standard price.

2. Gold coins

There are two types of gold coins — bullion type and numismatic type.

Bullion coins are gold coins that have a value determined, to a large extent, by their gold content. These coins trade at a very small premium over their actual price in relation to their gold content. Here are some of the more popular bullion coins:

Place of origin	Name of coin	Gold content
United States	American Eagle	1 oz.
United States	Double Eagle	1
Canada	Maple Leaf	1
Australia	Golden Nugget Koala	1
Austria	Corona	0.98
China	Panda	1
France	Britannia Napoleon	1
Mexico	Centenario	1.2056
South Africa	Krugerrand	1
Vienna	Philharmonic	1

Other bullion coins include the British sovereign (which has a higher premium), the Mexican 20, 10, 5 and 2½ peso coins, the Russian chevronetz and the South African ½, ¼, and ¹⁄₁₀ oz. Krugerrand coins. Maple Leaf, Golden Nugget Koala, Britannia Napoleon, and American Eagle also have ½, ¼, and ¹⁄₁₀ oz. versions.

Numismatic gold coins are those minted at a certain point in time and are currently available in limited quantities. They sell at a premium that may be considerably higher compared to their gold content.

The price of these coins is determined by several factors. Some of the major factors are:

(a) Number of coins originally minted

(b) Number of coins still in circulation

(c) Age of the coin

(d) Condition of the coin

Coins minted in limited quantities with limited current circulation and older coins in better condition will, in general, have a greater value than coins minted in large quantities with a large number still in circulation, or more recently minted coins in poor condition.

While this may sound logical, it can be difficult to evaluate these factors. How do you know the number of coins currently in circulation? How is good condition defined? A simple blemish in a numismatic coin, which may not be apparent to the buyer, may lower the value of a numismatic coin considerably.

3. Gold certificates

Gold certificates are issued by some banks and dealers. When you buy gold certificates you are, in effect, buying gold bullion. The company that sells you these certificates stores the gold on your behalf. The bullion is registered in your name. The commission charges could be as low as 0.25% or as high as 5%. In addition, the issuing company will charge you a modest storage fee. You can buy and sell gold this way without ever taking delivery. (You can, for instance, buy gold certificates through the Toronto-Dominion Bank.) In many cases, you will avoid bar charges which you are expected to pay when you actually take delivery.

4. Gold stocks

Buying shares in gold mining companies is another way you can participate in the gold market. There are several South African and Canadian mining companies whose shares are commonly traded. Some investors prefer not to buy South African gold stocks because of the current political situation there. Some of the factors that affect the stock prices are the current price of gold, the cost of production per ounce, the life of the mine, and management competence.

5. Gold futures

A futures contract obligates you to buy (or sell) a certain amount of gold at some specific time in the future at a price specified now. You may, however, liquidate the contract before that date. Gold futures are usually for 100 troy ounces. You may buy a futures contract if you expect the price of gold to rise before a specified date.

The main attraction of gold futures is that you pay only about 10% to 20% of the total value when you buy the contract. The rest is due when you take delivery. This gives you high leverage if the market moves according to your predictions. Since you are obligated to buy (or sell) at a given price, you could end up losing a lot more than your original investment if the market moves against you.

c. HOW YOU CAN INVEST IN GOLD

Of these five basic ways of owning gold, one is completely unsuited for the small investor: gold futures. This method can be very profitable. However, the small investor should avoid the temptation. When you buy futures, you can lose all your investment capital plus a lot more. Since the small investor's priority is to preserve the capital, futures are unsuitable.

The following methods are better suited for the small investor.

1. Gold bullion for the small investor

Until recently, the smallest gold bullion bar that could be purchased was a one-ounce bar. Such bars carry a premium of 10%, in addition to an assaying fee. They are also difficult to trade.

Some brokerage houses in the United States offer accounts that work like mutual funds. For example, you may want to invest $100 in gold. Your investment is pooled with that of other investors. Gold bullion is bought in bulk each day. The commission can be about 6% (or less if you invest more). Such plans do not carry a storage fee, assaying fee, insurance fee, or sales tax. The gold is retained by the brokerage house and you can sell it whenever you want.

2. Gold coins for the small investor

As discussed earlier, there are two types of gold coins — bullion type and numismatic type. Bullion coins are traded solely for their gold content. Numismatic coins are traded not only for their gold content but also for qualities such as rarity, age, condition, and appearance. The premium on numismatic coins can far exceed their gold value. The value of numismatic coins may often be unrelated to their gold content. Therefore, numismatic gold coins cannot be truly considered as gold investments.

There are several bullion coins. The most popular of these are the South African Krugerrand, the Canadian Maple Leaf, the U.S. Eagle, and, to a lesser extent, the Chinese Panda and the Mexican Onza.

(a) The Krugerrand

The Krugerrand contains exactly one troy ounce of gold. It has a fineness of .9167 or 22 karats. It is widely traded and carries a premium of 2% to 6% over the gold price. Krugerrands are traded throughout the world. The Krugerrand is legal tender in South Africa.

Smaller investors may be interested to know that Krugerrands are also available in fractional units. You can buy ½ oz., ¼ oz., or 1/10 oz. Krugerrands. However, these fractional units carry a much higher premium, as shown here:

83

Unit	Typical Premium%
1 oz. Krugerrand	4%
½ oz. Krugerrand	8
¼ oz. Krugerrand	12
⅒ oz. Krugerrand	18

Thus, if gold is selling at $400, buying ten ⅒ oz. Krugerrands will cost you about $60 more than buying a 1 oz. Krugerrand. For this reason, you should not buy fractional units unless you cannot afford to buy the 1 oz. Krugerrand.

(b) The Maple Leaf

The Canadian Maple Leaf also contains exactly one troy ounce of gold. It has a fineness of .999, or 24 karats. Although a latecomer to the scene, it is now widely accepted around the world. It carries a premium similar to that of the Krugerrand.

The 1 oz. Maple Leaf has a face value of $50 and is available in fractional units: ¼ oz. ($10 face value) and ⅒ oz. ($5 face value). The fractional units, as discussed before, carry a higher premium and hence are not recommended for the very small investor.

(c) The U.S. Eagle

The U.S. Eagle contains 91.67% pure gold, 5.33% copper and 3% silver. It is very popular in the United States. The Eagle is available in smaller denominations as well: ½ oz., ¼ oz., and ⅒ oz. The premium is slightly higher compared to that of the Maple Leaf.

(d) The Mexican Onza

This coin is similar to those described above. It contains one troy ounce of gold. Although less widely traded, the Mexican Onza carries a premium similar to that of the Krugerrand or the Maple Leaf.

(e) The Austrian and the Hungarian Crown

The 100 crown (Corona) coins produced by Austria and Hungary are much more popular than their other gold coins. The 100 Corona contains .9802 ounces of fine gold, making it slightly less valuable as bullion than the Krugerrand or the Maple Leaf. Corona coins are not legal tender. They are copies of coins issued by the former Austro-Hungarian Empire. The Austrian and the Hungarian Coronas are usually considered to be the same coin, and trade at the same price. The dealer premium for these coins is relatively low.

(f) The Vienna Philharmonic Gold Bullion Coin

The Philharmonic was one the world's best selling coins in 1995 and 1996. It contains 24 karats, or .999 ounces of fine gold. It comes in four different sizes: 1 oz., 1/2 oz., 1/4 oz., and 1/10 oz.

(g) The Mexican peso

Of all gold coins issued by Mexico, the 50-peso coin is the most popular. It contains 1.2057 ounces of fine gold. It was originally issued in 1921 to commemorate Mexico's 100th anniversary and therefore is also called the Centenario. In South America, the Centenario is the most popular gold coin. The coin is also traded in North America and in Europe. All Centenarios are dated copies of the original issue.

The Mexican 20-peso, which contains .48 ounces of gold, is less popular.

(h) The British sovereign

The British sovereign contains .2354 ounces of fine gold. It has been minted continuously since 1817. These are semi-numismatic coins, especially those minted in earlier years. Some coins carry premiums of up to 50% over their gold bullion value. The British sovereign bears the image of the reigning queen or king on one side and a scene of St. George slaying the dragon on the other. It is also legal tender in Britain. The sovereign is popular with both investors and numismatists.

(i) U.S. $20 Gold Double Eagles

These coins were struck between 1950 and 1933. Two types of Double Eagles are now in circulation — St. Gaudens and Liberty Head. These coins contain .97 troy ounces of gold and carry premiums up to 100%. These coins should be purchased in strictly uncirculated condition. However, even minted-state coins may bear "bag marks" (scratches) from being handled in bags.

3. Gold bullion accounts for the small investor

A gold bullion account is exactly like a savings account, except that deposits are converted into ounces of gold at the time of deposit. The value of your "savings" is determined by the daily prices of gold. (Please note these savings do not pay any interest; your gain or loss is solely determined by the price of the gold on the day you decide to sell.)

4. Gold funds for the small investor

Another way to participate in the gold market is to buy shares in gold mining companies. For a beginning investor, this has several disadvantages:

(a) Relatively high cost of quality mining stocks

(b) Commission for both buying and selling

(c) Possibility of a particular company being misman-aged

(d) Political climate affecting a particular company

A beginning investor needs an alternative that offers diversification, is cheaper, is safe, and carries no commissions. In fact, there is such an alternative. These are mutual funds that specialize in gold. These funds invest in gold (and other metals). Here are some no-load funds:

United States

American Cent Global Gold
American Century Funds
Box 419146
Kansas City, MO 64141-6146
Phone: 1-800-345-2021/(816) 531-5575
www.americancentury.com

Invesco Strat Port – Gold
INVESCO Funds Group Inc.
Box 173706
Denver, CO 80217
Phone: 1-800-675-1705/(303) 930-6300
www.invesco.com

Lexington GoldFund
Lexington Management Co.
80 Park W., Plaza 2
Saddlebrook, NJ 07663
Phone: 1-800-526-0057/(201) 845-7300

Scudder Gold
Scudder Funds
Box 2291
Boston, MA 02107-2291
Phone: 1-800-225-2470/(617) 295-1000
funds.scudder.com

Canada

Altamira Precious Metals
Altamira Investment Services
130 W. King Street, Suite 900
Toronto, ON M5X 1K9
Phone: 1-800-263-2824
Fax: (416) 203-7484
(Minimum investment: Initial: $1,000; Subsequent: $50)

CIBC Precious Metals Fund
CIBC Securities
200 W. King Street, 7th Floor
Toronto, ON M5H 4A8
Phone: 1-800-465-3863
Fax: (416) 351-4438
(Minimum investment: Initial: $1,000; Subsequent: $25)

First Canadian Precious Metals
First Canadian Mutual Funds
302 Bay Street, 10th Floor
Toronto, ON M5X 1A1
Phone: 1-800-665-7700
Fax: (416) 927-7210
(Minimum investment: Initial: $500; Subsequent: $50)

Green Line Precious Metals
TD Asset Management, Mutual Fund Services
Box 1, TD Centre
Toronto, ON M5K 1A2
Phone: 1-800-268-8166
Fax: (416) 944-5828
(Minimum investment: Initial: $2,000; Subsequent: $100)

Royal Trust Precious Metals Fund
Royal Mutual Funds
Box 7500, Station A
Toronto, ON M5W 1P9
Phone: 1-800-463-3863
Fax: 1-800-463-2926
(Minimum investment: Initial: $1,000; Subsequent: $25)

Scotia Precious Metals Fund
Scotia Securities
40 W. King Street, 5th Floor
Toronto, ON M5H 1H1
Phone: 1-800-268-9269
Fax: (416) 288-4455
(Minimum investment: Initial $500; Subsequent: $25)

12

HOW TO INVEST IN SILVER

a. WHY INVEST IN SILVER?

There are several reasons why a beginning investor should consider silver.

(a) Silver is poor man's gold. In the fall of 1998, you could have bought 58 ounces of silver for the price of one ounce of gold.

(b) Silver often rises in price when gold goes up.

(c) Silver is an industrial metal. There is always a demand for silver.

(d) Unlike gold, silver is used in many industries. So the price of silver should rise in the long term.

b. SOME COMMON WAYS TO PARTICIPATE IN THE SILVER MARKET

Similar to gold, there are basic ways to participate in the silver market. These are:

(a) Silver bullion

(b) Silver coins

(c) Silver certificates

(d) Silver stocks

(e) Silver options

(f) Silver futures

These ways of buying silver are exactly the same as their gold counterparts. For an explanation of the above methods, please refer to the chapter on gold.

c. HOW YOU CAN INVEST IN SILVER

Investing in silver is similar to investing in gold. Most dealers who deal in gold also deal in silver.

1. Silver bullion

You can pay cash and accept delivery of silver bullion. Common sizes of silver bars are 10 (troy) ounces, 100 ounces, and 1,000 ounces. Since there are several charges when you take delivery, you may be better off leaving the silver you purchase with your dealer until you decide to sell.

2. Silver coins

Silver coins are perhaps the best starting point for small investors interested in precious metals. Until 1965, the United States produced silver coins in several denominations: dollars, half dollars, quarters, and dimes. Such coins are referred to as *junk silver* and are now bought and sold mainly for their silver content.

Junk silver can be bought as bags or as rolls. A bag contains silver coins whose face value is $1,000. The silver contents of pre-1965 coins is approximately 720 ounces per bag. Each bag will cost approximately 720 x the current silver price per ounce. The high price makes it difficult for small investors to invest in bags. Rolls are a lower-cost alternative. Dimes come in rolls of 50, and quarters come in rolls of 40. The approximate cost is:

Dime rolls = 3.6 x the price per oz. of silver
Quarter rolls = 7.2 x the price per oz. of silver

There are also numismatic silver coins. For the beginning investor, however, junk silver still offers the best value. There are far too many silver coins from around the world that qualify for the title numismatic and are best left out of your portfolio until you become familiar with this market.

Junk silver can be bought from most of the coin dealers listed in the Resource Directory at the back of this book.

3. Silver bullion accounts

A silver bullion account works exactly like a gold bullion account (see chapter 11).

13

HOW TO INVEST IN REAL ESTATE

a. REAL ESTATE AND THE SMALL INVESTOR

You can make a fortune in real estate. But you need to be knowledgeable in buying a property and willing to spend the time to understand the market. I assume you do not want to spend a lot of time and that you do not want to get seriously involved in the real estate business. Even so, you can make money in a small way in real estate.

Get into real estate by all means, but only if you have some special knowledge. The reason for this is that real estate is highly leveraged. This means that you borrow a lot more than you currently have. If you buy a property for $100,000 and put down $10,000, you have borrowed $90,000. The only way you can make money is for the value of the property to go up. If it does not, you are paying interest on $90,000 year after year. This is not a position you want to be in if you are a small investor. So, I believe that small investors should not get into direct real estate investment unless they have some special knowledge in this area or know how to buy an under-valued property, add value to it by renovating, and then resell it. Since I don't expect most small investors to possess such special knowledge, I recommend you explore other ways to profit from real estate.

If at all possible, you should own your own home. Owning your home commits you to paying the mortgage, but you save on rent. If the value of your house goes up, you can make a tidy profit. In Canada, you do not pay capital gains tax when you sell your home. This makes owning your home very attractive. It is an investment you can keep using for your benefit until there is profit to be made.

b. REAL ESTATE INVESTMENT TRUSTS (REITs)

Real estate investment trusts (REITs) are companies that invest in apartment complexes, shopping malls, and other commercial and residential properties. When you buy shares (units) in these companies, you become a part-owner of this property.

In the United States, there are two types of REITs: REITs that actually own properties and REITs that lend money to real estate developers. REITs that own properties (equity-type) have tax advantages and therefore should be preferred to the mortgage-type REITs.

Shares in REITs can generally be bought or sold like shares in any corporation. If you are interested in this form of investment, write to:

National Association of REITs
1129 20th Street N.W., Suite 305
Washington, DC 20036-3482
Phone: 1-800-3NAREIT / (202) 785-8717
www.nareit.com

If you want to receive a list of REITs and would like to know more, request their REIT Fact Book and a current REIT list from the association. (There may be a small charge for this.)

In Canada there are hardly any REITs but the following are currently operating:

- Canadian REIT
- RealFund
- Riocan
- Summit

c. WHY INVEST IN REITs?

REITs normally aim to hold high-quality real estate. REITs pass on all income (untaxed) to unit holders. While you need to pay tax on the income you receive, you may also be eligible for preferential tax treatment (such as capital cost allowance and interest deductions). REITs provide instant diversification and professional management.

d. WHAT ELSE SHOULD YOU KNOW?

You should remember that investing in REITs does not automatically mean that you will make money. Much depends on the experience of management and economic conditions when you invest. Another thing you should know is that not all REITs are equally liquid, especially if the properties held by a REIT are not of good value. So do your homework and find out what is in their portfolio before you invest. If you are not sure, don't invest. Look for other options.

e. HOW TO BUY AND SELL REIT UNITS

REIT units are like stocks. To buy them, you should go through your stockbroker.

f. REAL ESTATE MUTUAL FUNDS

There are also mutual funds that invest in real estate (mostly commercial). They work exactly the same way as many other mutual funds. There are some differences though:

- The value of a real estate mutual fund is decided by an evaluation of the properties owned by the mutual fund. Evaluations and what one actually would get for a property are often two different things.

- Many real estate mutual funds evaluate their net asset value only once in three months. This makes buying and selling less immediate.

- Real estate funds can impose a moratorium on redemptions if they feel redemptions will harm the fund even further when the market is down.

If you are still interested, here are some no-load real estate mutual funds:

United States

- CGM Realty
- Columbia Real Estate Equity
- Fidelity Real Estate Investment

Canada

- CIBC Canadian Real Estate
- GWL Canadian Real Estate (G) NL
- Royal LePage Commercial

14

EVEN MORE WAYS TO MAKE MONEY

So far, we have discussed different types of investments that are safe for a small investor. There are, however, several other forms of investments that are highly profitable. These investments share one or more of the following characteristics:

(a) You need a *larger amount of money* to participate.

(b) You need greater *knowledge or experience* to participate.

(c) There are several *pitfalls* for the unwary investor.

Some of these investments are presented here. Because these investments can be quite complex, please consult other sources before investing your money.

a. HOW TO MAKE MONEY IN OPTIONS

1. Call option

A *call option* is the right to buy 100 shares of a specified stock, at a specified price before a specified date. The stock specified is the *underlying stock*; the price at which you have a right to buy is the *strike price*; the particular date on which your right to buy expires is the *expiration date*.

For example, IBM shares are trading at $140 in October. Suppose you expect the price to move up to at least $160 before January. Since it is too expensive to buy 100 shares of IBM ($140 x 100 = $14,000), you may buy a call option for about a $600 premium which gives you the right to buy 100 shares before January at $150 per share.

Since you have already paid a premium of $6 per share ($600 ÷ 100), IBM has to move up to at least $156 before January for you to make a profit (strike price + premium: $150 + $6 = $156). Beyond this break-even point, every dollar move-up results in a profit of $100 to you. Thus, on the expiration day, if IBM sells at $160, your profit will be $400 on an investment of just $600. This is a profit of nearly 67% in just three months! You may sell your option at the current market price at any time you wish.

What happens if IBM trades at or below $156 on the expiration date? You simply lose all the money you paid for the option — $600 plus commission. You cannot, however, lose more than this amount.

2. Put option

You can also buy a *put option*. A put option gives you the right to sell 100 shares of a particular stock at a specified price before a specified date. In the above example, if you predicted that IBM would go down by January, you would buy a put option. You would make money if the stock went down below the strike price. Otherwise, you would lose the premium paid.

3. The advantages of options

Options are attractive for these reasons:

- You can participate in the growth of high-price stocks with very little capital.

- Your maximum loss is predetermined.

The main disadvantage of options is that if your prediction does not materialize before the expiration date, you stand to lose all your investment plus commission.

However, there are several ways in which an option can be used effectively. For example, suppose in October you buy 100 shares of IBM which trade at $140. You can sell a call option which expires next January for, let's say, $1,100. This gives the buyer of the call option the right to buy from you 100 IBM shares at $140 before January. Between October and January, one of the following will happen.

(a) *IBM will go up steeply.* Should this happen, you will be asked to sell your shares at $140 per share. You get to keep $1,100 paid to you as a premium. Your profit for four months is equal to:

$$\frac{\text{Premium received}}{\text{Your investment during the period}} = \frac{1,100}{14,000} = 7.8\%$$

A return of 7.8% (or approximately 23.4% a year) is thus guaranteed.

(b) *IBM will move neither up nor down.* If the price of IBM remains more or less the same, you will not be asked to sell your shares. You keep the $1,100 you received and, upon expiry of the option, you can sell another option on the same stock for a future date. You can repeat the process and get steady income periodically. In addition, any dividend you receive is also yours to keep.

(c) *IBM will go down steeply.* Should this happen, you will not be asked to deliver the shares. However, should you wish to sell the shares and cut your losses before the expiration date, it would be safer to repurchase the option you sold before selling your shares.

Thus, the above strategy assumes a predetermined rate of return on your investment in a steady or a rising market and slightly lowers your losses in a declining market. (Please note that this strategy also limits your maximum profits in a sharply rising market.)

The strategy is both simple and conservative. There are several interesting ways to make money in options while at the same time limiting your risk. If this investment interests you, you should read at least one good book on the subject. You may want to start with a primer such as *Getting Started in Options* by Michael C. Thomsett (3rd edition, published by John Wiley & Sons, 1997).

Options are traded like stocks. Your stockbroker will be able to buy and sell options for you according to your requirements.

b. HOW TO MAKE MONEY IN COMMODITIES

Commodity futures are simply a way of betting. Suppose wheat is selling at $3.00 a bushel in May. You are convinced that by September, the price of wheat will be at least $3.50 a bushel. There is someone else in the marketplace who believes that the price will go down by September, probably to $2.50 a bushel. So you bet against each other — you agree to buy 5,000 bushels of wheat from the other person in September for $3.00; the other person agrees to sell it to you at that price.

You figure that if your prediction is correct, you stand to make a profit of 50¢ a bushel or $2,500 in all; the other person similarly figures that if the price goes down to $2.50, he will make a profit of 50¢ per bushel or $2,500 in all. If the price moves in either direction, one of you will gain and the other will lose a corresponding amount. In either case, the losing player just pays the winning player the difference, instead of actually buying or selling the wheat in question.

Although that is not the only use of commodity futures, most commodity futures are traded as described above. In actual practice, commodity trading has the following features:

- You do not directly bet with another player, you bet through a commodity broker. The broker, in turn, goes through a commodity exchange which is a central clearing house.

- Commodity trading is available only for certain grain, currencies, metals, and food products. When you bet (buy or sell a contract), you may do so only for a standard quantity (e.g., 5,000 bushels of wheat).

- When you bet, you have to put down a margin amount (a certain percentage of the total value of the contract). If the market moves against you, you may be asked to put down more money.

You may get out of the contract before the due date. Your profit or loss at this point will be determined by the market price of the contract.

You may, if you wish, take delivery of the commodity after the due date.

Obviously, just as you can buy a contract when you think the price will go up, you can also sell a contract. In this case, you agree to deliver the commodity (or pay the difference between the market price and the contract price) at a specified date. When you sell a contract, you assume that the price of the commodity will go down and you can profit by purchasing the contract at a lower price.

1. Disadvantages of commodity trading

Commodity trading requires considerable discipline. Many beginners lose all their capital during their first year of trading. At a minimum, you should —

(a) be able to control your greed when things go your way,

(b) be able to sleep soundly when you lose a few hundred dollars in a matter of hours, and

(c) resist overtrading.

2. Advantages of commodity trading

Because of the low margin requirement in commodity trading, it is possible to make large sums of money with a small amount of investment capital.

Commodities are a lot more volatile than other forms of investments. It is possible to make a quick fortune in commodities.

The rewards of commodity trading are high. While devastating losses are possible, for a disciplined trader it need be no more risky than trading in stocks and bonds. If you want to fully understand how this market works, Todd Lofton's *Getting Started in Futures* is a good book on the subject (3rd edition, published by John Wiley Ltd., 1997).

There are several commodity exchanges. In most exchanges, the contract sizes are large. There are, however, two exchanges that sell smaller contracts:

The MidAmerica Commodity Exchange
141 W. Jackson Boulevard
Chicago, IL 60604
Phone: (312) 435-3500
www.midam.com

The Winnipeg Commodity Exchange
360 Main Street, Suite 500
Winnipeg, MB R3C 3Z4
Phone: (204) 949-0495

Just as you need a stockbroker to trade in stocks, you need a commodity broker to trade in commodities. Most large brokerage houses also deal in commodities. It is unwise to deal in commodities if you have less than $5,000 to $10,000 as risk capital. Many commodity brokerage firms will not even deal with small investors.

One final piece of advice: if you are a small investor, start with grain futures where the losses are smaller. Avoid trading in metals and currencies until you have a sufficiently large amount of capital.

c. HOW TO MAKE MONEY IN ART AND COLLECTIBLES

Works of art and collectibles are risky as investments. They may decline in value drastically, you may not find a ready market when you want to sell them, and, unless you are careful, you may end up paying inflated prices when you buy.

On the positive side, art and collectibles are pleasurable to own. They may appreciate in value more than any of your other investments, and, if you invest wisely, it is unlikely that you will incur any great loss over a long period of time.

1. What to do

If you are interested in investing in art and collectibles, you should follow these guidelines:

(a) *Specialize.* Collectibles include art, antiques, Chinese ceramics, diamonds, books, stamps, and a variety of other items. Choose an area you feel comfortable with and get to know as much as possible about the field.

(b) *Buy what you like to own.* Since most collectibles tend to be long-term investments, you may have to live with what you bought. You might as well buy something that gives you pleasure while you have it.

(c) *Avoid fads.* Fads, by definition, change. Do not rush to buy fad items. Fads change quickly and you may be stuck with something that is worthless from an investment point of view.

(d) *Buy quality.* Quality items keep their value while nonquality items are unpredictable. Concentrate on quality.

(e) *Buy collectibles that have large markets.* Some collectibles are highly specialized and only a handful of investors are interested. This type of investment is highly illiquid. Avoid such collectibles.

(f) *Get a certificate of authenticity.* When you buy a collectible, get a dealer's certificate of title, guarantee of
authenticity, and registration.

(g) *Know the current market price before buying.* To avoid
costly impulse purchases, you should investigate the
current price range for the collectible you want to
buy. You should also decide in advance the maximum price you are willing to pay.

(h) *Buy through reputable dealers.* Because fakes and
worthless collectibles abound in the marketplace, try
to buy only through reputable dealers.

2. How to get started

Sotheby's and Christie's are two of the most reputable auction houses for collectibles. Both of these firms publish catalogues through the year, giving detailed descriptions of the
items that will be available at forthcoming auctions. These
catalogues give the estimated prices of the items. You may
send in your bid for any item you like. At the time of auction,
the company will bid on your behalf so that, if you are
successful, you will get the best possible price. You may wish
to contact:

Sotheby's
1334 York Avenue
New York, NY 10021
Phone: (212) 606-7000
www.sothebys.com

Sotheby's (Canada) Inc.
9 Hazelton Avenue
Toronto, ON M5R 2E1
Phone: (416) 926-1774

Christie's Fine Art Auctioneers
502 Park Avenue
New York, NY 10022
Phone: (212) 546-1000
www.christies.com

Christie's Fine Art Auctioneers
170 W. Bloor Street, Suite 210
Toronto, ON M5S 1T9
Phone: (416) 960-2063

d. HOW TO MAKE MONEY IN TAX SHELTERS

We pay taxes on a graduated scale. As your income increases, you keep less and less of the additional money you earn. Although, overall, you may pay only 25% or 30% of your income as taxes, the marginal tax rate could be 40% or higher. This means that, at your level of income, you have to pay at least $40 in taxes for every extra $100 you earn.

For an investor this above fact is very important. Suppose you can save $3,000 a year. If you do not have to pay taxes on this, then you have $3,000 to invest. If you could get an 18% return on this amount, your savings would be worth more than $1 million in 25 years.

On the other hand, if you were to pay taxes at 40% on your savings of $3,000 a year, the total value of your investment at the end of 25 years would be $400,000 less. By planning your finances properly, you can reduce your tax bill, thus making more money available for your investments. Legal ways of avoiding taxes are usually referred to as tax shelters.

Tax shelters are usually of two types: *tax deferred* and *tax free*. Tax deferred investments enable you to postpone the taxes to a future date, while tax-free investments enable you to avoid taxes completely. Both these types of investments should be considered seriously. If they apply to you, you should take advantage of them.

Several readers have written to me with their comments and suggestions since the first edition of this book. I have tried to respond to their suggestions in this edition. I have been unable to respond as fully as I would like to requests from readers for information on tax shelters. I am unable to include much information on taxes because tax rules can change very rapidly. What I write may become outdated by the time you read the book.

My general suggestion is to make use of tax shelters and retirement plans such as RRSP (Canada) and IRA and Keogh (United States) whenever you can. My only caution is that *you should not invest in just anything because it is a tax shelter.* If it is not a sound investment, it is not a good buy just because it shelters your money from taxes.

Because taxes can affect the value of your investments, make sure you read some good books on the subject. Be sure that the books you read are not outdated. I urge you to find out as much as you can because this is a very important topic for small investors.

How do you compare tax-free investments with taxable investments? Let's say, for example, that a tax-free investment yields a 6% return and a taxable investment yields a 10% return. Which one should you choose? To compare the two, do the following calculation:

$$(100 - \frac{\text{Tax-free yield}}{\text{Taxable yield}}) \ \times 100$$

In our example:

$$(100 - \frac{6}{10}) \ \times 100 = 40\%$$

This means your *marginal* tax (the tax you pay on the last dollar you earn) should be at least 40%, for it to be worthwhile.

e. HOW TO MAKE MONEY WITH SWISS BANK ACCOUNTS

A Swiss bank account is not just for the rich. It offers so many advantages that it is suitable even if you are a small investor. Let us consider some of the advantages.

1. Security

Swiss currency is one of the strongest in the world. In most countries the rate of inflation is so high it erodes the purchase power of the money you save. In Switzerland, on the other hand, the rate of inflation has been traditionally low.

2. Privacy

There are strict laws governing the secrecy of your account. In Switzerland, it is illegal for a bank to divulge information about your account to anyone, including the Swiss government. (This, however, may not protect a customer when he or she indulges in fraudulent activities.)

3. Services

Swiss banks provide a wide variety of services to their customers. Unlike our banks in North America, Swiss banks can help you convert your currencies into Euro currency, buy stocks and bonds on your behalf, store gold and silver, and perform similar financial management services. The range of services offered by Swiss banks is indeed impressive.

4. Swiss bank account

Although many Swiss banks require a large minimum amount to open an account, some cater to small investors. To get started, write to the banks listed in the Resource Directory under Swiss Banks, and ask for an application to open a Swiss franc savings account. Once you open an account, you can mail checks drawn on a U.S. or Canadian bank. All correspondence can be conducted in English.

15

LOW-RISK STRATEGIES FOR HIGHER PROFITS

Most investors look for two things —

- safety of their capital, and

- increased return on their investments.

You can use specific strategies to get what you want. A strategy is a method that is well thought out in advance. You follow the strategy, even when things don't seem rosy. A strategy helps you avoid panic reactions when things don't go your way.

a. STRATEGY 1: DOLLAR COST AVERAGING

Let us suppose that —

(a) you want to invest a specific amount on a regular basis,

(b) you want to invest over a long period of time, and

(c) you are interested in high-quality, dividend-paying stock.

There is no guarantee that the stocks will increase in value over any given period of time. For example, assume that in 1970 you bought $1,000 worth of stocks in each of the following ten prominent companies. Their worth on January 2, 1980, was:

Name of company	Stock value in 1970	Stock value in 1980
Eastman Kodak	$1,000	$584
General Foods	1,000	809
General Motors	1,000	723
Goodyear	1,000	419
IBM	1,000	883
Sears	1,000	589
Texaco	1,000	942
U.S. Steel	1,000	778
Westinghouse	1,000	692
Woolworth	1,000	665
	$10,000	$7,084

Ignoring the dividends for the time being, the investment is worth 30% *less* than it was ten years before. (If you take inflation into account, the investments are worth less than 50% of the 1970 value.)

During the 1987 stock market crash, the value of many stocks plummeted. Suppose you had bought blue chip stocks immediately after the crash. After three years (October 1990) would your investment have appreciated sharply? The answer is no!

Thus, it is clear that even if you invest in blue chip companies, you need a good strategy to protect your investments.

Dollar cost averaging is one of the most widely known systems, and it achieves superior results under certain conditions. This system works best when you invest in high-quality dividend-paying stocks on a regular basis.

Dollar cost averaging involves purchasing the same dollar amount of stock at regular intervals, regardless of the price of the stock at the time of each purchase. For example, you may decide to buy $1,000 worth of TD Bank shares each year. Suppose you had done this for ten years, e.g., 1971 to 1980.

Amount invested = $1,000 per year

Year	Share price	Shares bought	Total no. shares	Estimated dividends
1971	$12.31	81	81	$30.00
1972	15.92	63	144	63.00
1973	19.38	56	200	100.00
1974	17.38	58	258	158.00
1975	19.75	51	309	216.00
1976	18.63	54	363	258.00
1977	16.80	60	423	321.00
1978	21.25	47	470	400.00
1979	21.63	36	506	614.00
1980	32.00	31	537	755.00
	$195.05			$2,915.00

Average share price = $195.05 ÷ 10 years = $19.50

Total dividend received = $2,915.00

By investing the same amount regularly, you were able to buy more shares when the prices were low. At the end of ten years, the average price paid per share was only $19.50 although the share price was $32 on October 31, 1980. In addition, you also received nearly 30% of your capital ($2,915) back in dividends.

As time goes by, the dividends also become very important. For example, by the end of the tenth year, the dividend received from TD Bank is equal to 75% ($755) of the annual investment! You can, of course, increase the profit by reinvesting the dividends in addition to making your regular investment.

- Dollar cost averaging is a system suitable for regular investors over a long period of time. It works best with dividend-paying, high-quality stocks.

- The system involves investing the same amount in the same stock periodically.

- In general, it may be said that dollar cost averaging is a simple system based on sound principles and is suitable for regular long-term investing.

When you invest the same amount in mutual funds at regular intervals, you are in fact using the dollar cost averaging method indirectly.

b. STRATEGY 2: THE RIGS STRATEGY

RIGS stands for Recession, Inflation, Growth, and Safety (or Speculation). RIGS is simply an automatic way of investing according to a formula. RIGS is a conservative long-term strategy for investing. By using this strategy, you can expect to earn approximately 14% to 16% per year (on average) on your long-term investments. (This is based on past experience with the strategy; it is not a guarantee.)

The basis of this strategy is the observation that economic conditions go in cycles and different investments do well under different economic conditions. During inflationary times, real estate, gold, and other tangibles do well; during recessionary periods, bonds, cash, and cash equivalents do well, and during growth periods, stocks and real estate do well. RIGS uses the following investments:

R-type investments

- Bonds

- Cash

- Cash equivalents

- Mortgage-backed securities

I-type investments

- Gold

- Real estate

- Other tangibles

G-type investments

- Common stocks
- Real estate

Some investors try to predict what is likely to happen in the future and invest accordingly. This can be risky when predictions go wrong. The RIGS strategy tries to avoid the risk by assuming that the future is not predictable, but even so money can be made. The strategy works as follows:

(a) Divide your money into three equal parts. (Example: You have $9,000 to invest. Divide it into three parts of $3,000 each.)

(b) Invest one-third of your money in R-type investments. (Example: Invest $3,000 in bonds or income mutual funds.)

(c) Invest one-third of your money in I-type investments. (Example: Invest $3,000 in gold, silver, or real estate, or in mutual funds that invest in any of these investments.)

(d) Invest one-third of your money in G-type investments. (Example: Invest $3,000 in stocks or equity mutual funds.)

(e) Whenever you have money to invest during the year, invest an equal amount in each type of investment (R,I, and G). If you save monthly, rotate your investment among the three types.

(f) At the end of the year, some of these investments would have gone up; some would have gone down. (Example: Let us assume that, by the year-end, R-type investments are worth $3,600, I-type investments $2,900, and G-type investments are worth $3,400, for a total of $9,900.)

(g) Rearrange your investments so that each type is worth the same dollar amount. (Example: Your investments are worth $9,900 by the year-end. You rearrange your investments so that each type — R, I, and G — has the same dollar value: $3,300. You do this by selling some of the R- and G-type investments and buying some I-type investments to bring every investment to the same dollar value.)

Once set up, this strategy needs very little attention. It works because it forces the investor to sell high and buy low every year. This strategy works well in the long term. It will not make money every single year, but when you take any five years (approximately one business cycle), the RIGS strategy has performed consistently well. By using this strategy, you can expect to make around 14% to 16% per year over a five-year period. This is not a guarantee, but a reasonable expectation based on past experience. You may occasionally find that all three investments have gone down. There is no need to panic. The investments will resume their growth soon enough.

The Investors Association of Canada (IAC) has a special report called *RIGS: The Strategy for Investing,* which explains in simple terms what the strategy is, how it works, and how you can set up your own investment program. You can get a copy of this brief report from IAC for $13.50 plus $2 for postage. Write to:

Investors Association of Canada
26 Soho Street, Suite 380
Toronto, ON M5T 1Z7

16

HIGHER-RISK STRATEGIES FOR HIGHER PROFITS

The profitability of some of the investments already discussed can be further increased by using a variety of special techniques. Although these techniques have the potential to increase your profits quite considerably, they usually require a large capital outlay to begin with. Hence, these systems should be used only when you have sufficient capital. You should also keep in mind that these are long-term strategies.

The two strategies discussed in this chapter are based on switching between investments. They require some understanding of how financial markets work. You may find them useful halfway through your investment program. They are here only for your reference.

a. STRATEGY 1: STOCK MARKET– MONEY MARKET SWITCH

This strategy is based on the observation that whenever interest rates go down, the stock market goes up; conversely, whenever interest rates go up, the stock market goes down. While this relationship is not perfect, it is still strong enough for us to benefit by it.

There are several systems that take advantage of this relationship. One such system is described below:

(a) Calculate the 39-week moving average for a given stock market fund. (A 39-week moving average is simply the average price of the fund's share for the previous 39 weeks.)

(b) If the current price of the fund is lower than the moving average, switch your money from the stock market fund to a money market fund.

(c) Continue plotting moving averages for the stock fund. When the current price of the stock fund goes above the moving average, switch all your investments back from the money market fund to the stock fund.

Following such a system increases the probability of being in the stock market when it is going up and being in the money market when the stock market is going down.

If you are interested in using such a system, but do not want to spend the time calculating moving averages, you may want to subscribe to one of the following newsletters which does the work for you and advises you when to switch. (Always call or write first and ask for a complimentary copy of the newsletter before subscribing.)

Fund Exchange
Paul A. Merriman and Associates
700-1200 N. Westlake Avenue
Seattle, WA 98109-3530
Phone: (206) 285-8877

Market Timer Report
Box 6244
Charlottesville, Virginia 22906
www.mtreport.com

Switch Fund Timing
Box 25430
Rochester, NY 14625
Phone: (716) 385-3122

If you use this system, make sure that both your money market and stock market funds are run by the same group, that they are no-load funds, and that the funds offer telephone switching privileges.

b. STRATEGY 2: GOLD–SILVER SWITCH

The prices of gold and silver usually go up and down at the same time. Sometimes, however, the price of gold rises faster than silver; at other times, the price of silver rises faster than gold. The following table shows the price relationship between gold and silver over a four-year period.

	Gold price (per oz.)	Silver price (per oz.)	Number of oz. of silver per one oz. of gold
Year 1			
Quarter 1	$240	$8.66	28
Quarter 2	281	10.07	28
Quarter 3	399	20.61	19
Quarter 4	524	40.41	13
Year 2			
Quarter 1	490	14.50	34
Quarter 2	662	16.81	39
Quarter 3	670	20.70	32
Quarter 4	589	15.80	37
Year 3			
Quarter 1	514	11.95	43
Quarter 2	421	8.58	49
Quarter 3	432	9.04	48
Quarter 4	400	8.20	49
Year 4			
Quarter 1	320	7.07	45
Quarter 2	314	5.73	55
Quarter 3	396	8.20	48
Quarter 4	442	10.50	42

Thus, at the end of the first quarter of the first year, 28 oz. of silver bought 1 oz. of gold; at the end of the last quarter of the same year, as little as 13 oz. of silver bought 1 oz. of gold. Yet by the second quarter of the fourth year, 1 oz. of gold bought more than four times as much silver!

Because the silver-gold ratio has fluctuated historically, it is reasonable to expect that it will continue to do so in the future.

To capitalize on this fact, you can set up a simple strategy. Simply keep the dollar values of gold and silver equal. This is best explained by an example. In this example, an investor buys $10,000 worth of gold and $10,000 worth of silver. Every three months the investor calculates the current values of gold and silver and readjusts the dollar amounts such that 50% of the total amount is invested in gold and the remaining 50% in silver. This is how it works:

First Quarter

Price of gold — $500 per oz.

Price of silver — $20 per oz.

Invest $10,000 in gold (10,000 ÷ 500) = 20 oz. of gold.

Invest $10,000 in silver (10,000 ÷ 20) = 500 oz. of silver.

Second Quarter

Price of gold — $600 per oz.

Price of silver — $15 per oz.

Now the value of the holdings is:

Gold — 20 oz. x $600 = $12,000

Silver — 500 oz. x $15 =   7,500
Total: $19,500

The investor wants to keep 50% ($19,500 ÷ 2 = $9,750) in silver and 50% in gold. Accordingly, $2,250 worth of gold

($12,000 - $9,750) is exchanged for $2,250 worth of silver. At this stage the investor has:

$9,750 ÷ $600 = 16.25 oz. of gold

$9,750 ÷ $15 = 650 oz. of silver

Third Quarter

Price of gold — $700

Price of silver — $20

Value of holdings:

Gold — $700 x 16.25 oz. = $11,375

Silver — $20 x 650 oz. =   13,000

Total: $24,375

Once again the investments are rearranged so that 50% of the total amount is invested in silver and the other 50% in gold.

By now it should be obvious how the system works. Because gold went up in price during the second month and silver went down, silver was cheap in relation to gold. Consequently, gold was exchanged for silver. Subsequently, silver went back to its initial price while gold continued to climb. The total profit is now $4,375. An investor who did not follow this procedure would have made a profit of $4,000 (i.e., $700 x 20 oz. + $20 x 500 oz. = $24,000), which is about 2% less profit. Over a number of years, that 2% difference would be substantial in terms of a dollar amount.

This is, of course, an artificial example. If you apply the principle to the actual data given earlier, it would look like the chart on the next page:

Date	Gold (oz.)	Silver (oz.)
Year 1		
Quarter 1	41.7	1,155
Quarter 2	41.7	1,155
Quarter 3	50.7	981
Quarter 4	63.2	819
Year 2		
Quarter 1	43.7	1,477
Quarter 2	40.6	1,599
Quarter 3	45.0	1,457
Quarter 4	42.0	1,567
Year 3		
Quarter 1	39.2	1,687
Quarter 2	36.8	1,818
Quarter 3	37.4	1,788
Quarter 4	37.0	1,806
Year 4		
Quarter 1	38.5	1,740
Quarter 2	35.1	1,924
Quarter 3	37.5	1,809
Quarter 4	40.2	1,694

That is, over four years, 1.5 oz. of gold were parlayed into 539 oz. of silver without adding any more money!

17

HOW TO GET INFORMATION AT LOW OR NO COST

Investment books can be expensive. But there are several sources of free information. As a small investor, you should make use of them whenever possible. But please remember, if you write for information from people who want to sell you something (such as stockbrokers and insurance companies), you are likely to get telephone calls from them. If you do not want to buy what they are trying to sell, be firm and say no. They can be very persuasive!

Many financial writers and consumer columnists often mention free booklets on investments. Such publications are often advertised. Some of these are published by industry associations to promote the industry, some by large companies for prestige and others by companies that hope you will do business with them. They can be very useful but not necessarily unbiased. Throughout this book, I have referred to several publications. In this chapter, I would like to give you the names of some useful publications that can be obtained free of charge.

Not all free publications are good, *but some of them are excellent.* In fact, some of the best information included in this book came to my attention through free publications. How do you tell a good publication from a bad one? It's not easy. All I can say is, do not get carried away by what you read. Do not feel that you will miss a golden opportunity unless you act as these publications tell you. *Opportunities will always be*

119

there for an intelligent investor. As you gain experience, you will be able to discard bad advice.

In the meantime, use these publications to educate yourself at no cost. Exposure to different publications — even if some of them are bad — will make you a better investor.

a. U.S.–BASED MUTUAL FUNDS

You can get a number of free brochures on mutual funds from:

The Investment Company Institute
1401 H Street N.W.
Washington, DC 20005
Phone: (202) 326-5800
www.ici.org

Here are some of the free brochures offered:

- *Frequently Asked Questions About Mutual Fund Fees*
- *Frequently Asked Questions About Stock Mutual Funds*
- *A Guide to Closed-End Funds*
- *A Guide to Understanding Mutual Funds*
- *Questions You Should Ask Before Investing in Mutual Funds*

For $8.50, you can also get the *Guide to Mutual Funds*, which contains fund names, addresses, telephone numbers (many toll free), each fund's assets, initial and subsequent minimums, fees charged, where to buy, and other details. The introductory text serves as a short course in mutual fund investing.

b. CANADIAN MUTUAL FUNDS

In Canada, the Investment Fund Institute of Canada has several brochures available to the investing public free of charge.

- *Anatomy of a Mutual Fund*

- *Answers to the 10 Most Frequently Asked Questions About Mutual Funds*

- *Buying and Selling Mutual Funds*

- *Important Information Regarding Derivatives*

- *Leveraging*

- *A Smart Investment for a Child's Education*

In addition, you can receive, on a quarterly basis, the performance of most Canadian mutual funds. These *Performance Tables* show one-, three-, five-, and ten-year performance figures for hundreds of Canadian mutual funds. Also free is the *Member Directory*, which is actually the names, addresses, and phone numbers of mutual fund companies that are members of the Investment Funds Institute of Canada. If you would like to receive an information package, please contact:

The Investment Funds Institute of Canada
151 Yonge Street, 5th Floor
Toronto, ON M5C 2W7
Phone: (416) 363-2158
www.mutfunds.com/ific

c. OTHER PUBLICATIONS

The list given above is probably the most useful for the beginning investor. But a number of useful publications are available from other sources. A beginning investor should obtain these publications and become familiar with different aspects of investing.

Almost all stock exchanges have publications that are helpful to investors. The names and addresses of North American exchanges are given in the Resource Directory at the end of this book. You may want to write to them and ask for any publications that will help the individual investor.

Several industry associations also offer useful publications on taxation, executorship, and related topics. You may want to contact them for more information about the booklets that they make available to the general public.

United States

American Association of Individual Investors
625 N. Michigan Avenue
Chicago, IL 60611
Phone: 1-800-428-2244
www.aaii.org

American Association of Retired Persons
601 E Street N.E.
Washington, DC 20049
Phone: 1-800-424-3410
www.aarp.org

International Association for Financial Planning
5775 Glenridge Drive N.E., Suite B-300
Atlanta, GA 30328-5364
Phone: (404) 845-0011
www.iafp.org

National Association of Investors Corporation
Box 220
Royal Oak, MI 48068
Phone: (248) 583-6242
www.better-investing.org

Canada

Canadian Association of Financial Planners
439 University Avenue, Suite 1710
Toronto, ON M5G 1Y8
Phone: (416) 593-6592
www.cafp.org

Canadian Association of Retired Persons
227 E. Queen Street, Suite 1304
Toronto, ON M5C 2M6
Phone:(416) 363-8748

Canadian Investor Protection Fund
Royal Bank Plaza, South Tower, Suite 2400
Toronto, ON M5J 2J4
Phone: (416) 866-8366
www.cipf.ca

CGA of Ontario
240 E. Eglinton Avenue
Toronto, ON M4P 1K8
Phone: (416) 322-6520

Comp. Corp. (insurance industry)
1 E. Queen Street, Suite 1600
Toronto, ON M5C 2X9
Phone: (416) 359-2001
www.compcorp.ca

d. HOW TO GET EVEN MORE FREE PUBLICATIONS

The above list is by no means complete. There are literally hundreds of publications on investments available. Not all of them are good. Some are very self-serving. A beginner may have difficulty distinguishing a good publication from a biased one. I would suggest that you get as many free publications as possible and go through them. But do not be in a hurry to act upon their suggestions. Gradually, you will be able to tell the facts from a mere sales pitch.

You can develop your own list of free publications through several sources:

(a) Regularly go through consumer columns in your daily newspaper; free publications are often mentioned in them.

(b) Go through the advertisements in the business section of your daily newspaper; free publications on investments are advertised in this section from time to time.

(c) Write to industry associations (e.g., Investment Company Institute for No-Load Mutual Funds Association, The Gold Institute, etc.) and stock exchanges requesting information. You are likely to receive several useful publications.

PART IV
REALIZING YOUR DREAM: FINANCIAL FREEDOM

18
FUNDAMENTALS OF FINANCIAL GROWTH

After reading this far, you might still be wondering how to achieve financial freedom on $5 a day. It is all well and good to list the available opportunities, but how exactly should a beginner go about devising a plan to achieve financial freedom? I will describe a typical plan in the following chapter; but, before that, you need to understand some fundamentals of diversified long-term investments.

a. COMPOUND INTEREST

Even a modest amount, like $5 a day, when invested regularly over a long period, will gradually grow into a modest fortune. For example, $5 a day invested at 15% return will grow into $1 million in 35 years (see Chart #3).

Note how your savings grow slowly at the beginning and rapidly in later years. Time is an important element in making your money grow.

b. DIVERSIFIED INVESTMENTS

When your investments are diversified, the maximum you can lose on any one investment is 100%. The maximum gain, on the other hand is theoretically unlimited.

For example, if all you have is $10,000 in stocks, your stocks can go down in value and create losses for you. If, on the other hand, you have some stocks, some bonds, some gold, and some money market funds, it is very unlikely that all your investments will go down and stay down. As a

CHART #3
FUTURE VALUE — $150 SAVED MONTHLY
Interest compounded monthly

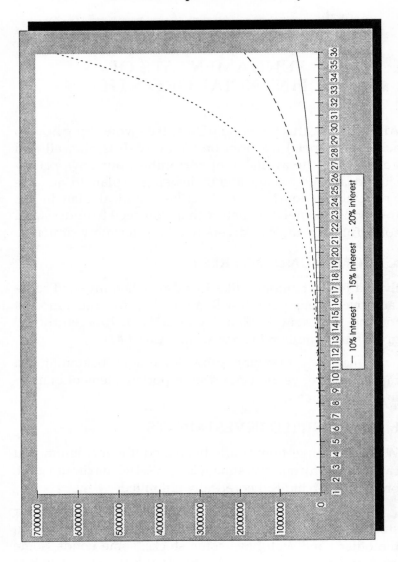

— 10% Interest -- 15% Interest ·· 20% interest

matter of fact, when some types of investments are down, others tend to move up. For example, when interest rates go up, the price of bonds goes down, but you get to make more money in money market funds.

Another advantage of having diversified investments is that one of these investments may go up dramatically in the next 10 to 15 years: for instance, gold quadrupled in value in the late seventies and early eighties; oil prices doubled during the Persian Gulf crisis in 1990. The stock market soared during the years 1982–87. The same holds true for the other investments that you build up. In a long-term diversified portfolio, the probability of growth is much greater than the probability of decline.

c. ECONOMIC CHANGES

Over a 10- to 15-year period, economic conditions change. Stock markets, gold, silver, foreign currencies, art, and collectibles go up and down. For example, during the 1984–85 year, bond prices went up by over 40%. By switching investments at appropriate times (see chapter 19), you can increase the return on investments appreciably.

d. CYCLES

The value of investments follows recurring patterns. At different points in time, different investments are favored by investors. These patterns are at times related to economic changes. While some people believe that such cycles can be predicted, long-term investors do not have to predict these. It is enough to know that cycles exist and to take advantage of the cycles when they occur.

e. FADS, PANICS, AND MASS HYSTERIA

From time to time, groups of people tend to act irrationally. Such irrationality and panic tend to dramatically increase the value of a specific investment to unreasonable levels for a short period of time. If we just watch for these moments we can profit handsomely. For example, in 1979–1980, gold doubled in price in six weeks; silver tripled in price in four months! Oil prices tripled in one year during 1974–75. Whenever these unusual events happen, you should cash in most of your holdings and wait for prices to come down. This strategy will increase the value of your investments considerably.

Over a long period (about 10 to 15 years), it is almost certain that each one of these five factors will operate in the marketplace, thereby making financial freedom a virtual certainty. All you need to do is to arrange your investments in such a way as to take maximum advantage of these factors when they materialize. This strategy is explained further in the next chapter.

19

A BLUEPRINT
FOR FINANCIAL FREEDOM

As mentioned earlier, even if you invest just $5 a day in the best possible way and do nothing else, you may be able to achieve financial freedom. But this will take a long time. If you wish to achieve financial freedom within a reasonable length of time (i.e., 10 to 15 years), I suggest that you follow the example of Mr. Keen Investor given below.

Mr. Keen Investor has no savings but he is intelligent and keen. He is willing to put the principles explained in this book into practice. He is willing to increase his savings by 20% each year whenever he can. This is how he goes about doing it.

a. PHASE 1: YEARS ONE TO THREE

Mr. Keen Investor is committed to saving $5 a day. In addition he is willing to add part of his annual salary increase, bonus, windfall money, and unexpected savings. He decides that every time his savings reach $100 he will invest it. This is what his calculations look like:

Year 1:	$5.00 a day to a total of $1,825.00 or approximately	18 x $100.00
Year 2:	$6.00 a day to a total of $2,190.00 or approximately	22 x $100.00
Year 3:	$7.20 a day to a total of $2,628.00 or approximately	26 x $100.00
		66 x $100.00

(Mr. Keen Investor figures that even if he can save only $5 a day during the second and third years, he can still add about 20% by other means.)

Mr. Keen Investor is conservative in his strategy and wants to diversify his investments without risking his capital. This is how he invests:

First	$100	Stock Funds	(SF)
Second	$100	Bond Funds	(BF)
Third	$100	Money Funds	(MF)
Fourth	$100	Foreign Funds	(FF)
Fifth	$100	Gold Funds	(GF)
Sixth	$100	Real Estate Funds	(RF)

After one year of saving $5 a day and investing it in the above program, his investments look like this:

SF	BF	MF	FF	GF	RF
$300	$300	$300	$300	$300	$300

This constitutes one block in Mr. Keen Investor's program. For the first three years, he decides to repeat investing in the same way. Thus, at the end of three years he expects his three blocks to look like the diagram below.

	SF	BF	MF	FF	GF	RF
Year 1	$300	$300	$300	$300	$300	$300
Year 2	$360	$360	$360	$360	$360	$360
Year 3	$440	$440	$440	$440	$440	$440

In other words, his total investments are:

SF	BF	MF	FF	GF	RF
$1,100	$1,100	$1,100	$1,100	$1,100	$1,100

Although Mr. Keen Investor saved about $6,600 in the first three years, his investments have grown in value because of interest he has received from money market funds, dividends he has received from stock market and real estate funds, and a modest appreciation on his other investments. He finds that some of these investments have appreciated modestly, some have depreciated modestly, some have appreciated considerably, and so on. At the end of three years, his investments are worth $8,800.

b. PHASE 2: YEARS FOUR TO SIX

Mr. Keen Investor is now satisfied that he has a sound base from which to move to the second phase of the program. He decides to redistribute the $8,800 he has at this stage as follows:

Stock Funds	$2,000
Bond Funds	2,000
Gold Funds	1,000
Real Estate Funds	1,000
Foreign Funds	1,000
Money Funds	1,000

He still has $800 left. He decides to invest this amount in more potentially rewarding (and risky) investments like art, collectibles, and call options.

In addition, Mr. Keen Investor continues his investment program by regularly investing an amount that is about 20% higher than the previous year. During the first three years, his block consisted of six units. From now on, Mr. Keen Investor decides to add one more unit to the block — risky investments (RI). His investment blocks for this phase look like this:

First	$100	Stock Funds (SF)
Second	$100	Bond Funds (BF)

Third	$100	Money Funds (MF)
Fourth	100	Foreign Funds (FF)
Fifth	100	Gold Funds (GF)
Sixth	100	Real Estate Funds (RF)
Seventh	100	Risky Investments (RI)

While continuing the basic program. Mr. Keen Investor decides that, by now, his investments are sufficiently diversified and he could increase his profits even more by using advanced techniques. The RIGS strategy (see chapter 15) especially appeals to him. He likes the fact that it is a safe and sensible strategy and very easy to use.

Regular savings, diversification, and the use of the RIGS technique help Mr. Keen Investor to achieve high returns on his investment. His total net worth at this point has increased to about $35,000. With this solid foundation, Mr. Keen Investor is ready to start the third phase of his investment program.

c. PHASE 3: YEARS SEVEN TO TEN

Mr. Keen Investor continues to save and invest regularly. He decides at this stage to continue to invest in high-risk areas like commodity futures, art, collectibles, and options and sets aside $5,000 for this purpose.

He continues with the program and continues with the RIGS strategy. He speculates with some of his money, but has the bulk of his capital in solid investments. Mr. Keen Investor ignores day-to-day fluctuations in the value of his investments. He knows he is investing for the long haul and feels comfortable about his strategy.

As years go by, Mr. Keen Investor is very pleased with the results. Sometimes his investments are up, sometimes they are down. But there is no doubt that his plan has been working. His total average return on investment has exceeded 15% per year. In addition, he has been able to take advantage of sudden

134

price surges in gold, silver, etc. By the 10th year, his net worth has increased to more than $100,000.

He diligently continues investing while watching his systems make money for him. By the 15th year, Mr. Keen Investor has well over $300,000. "Well, I am financially independent now," he muses. "It is only a question of time — maybe five or six years — before I turn this into $1 million or more."

Not bad for someone who started with $5 a day 15 years earlier.

Now back to reality. The scenario described above has been constructed on the basis of historical rates of return on investments, taking into account the factors that affect investments over a 10- to 15-year period. You may, in the next 15 years, do much better or you may do somewhat worse than he did. (It is unlikely that you will do much worse as long as you are a disciplined investor.)

In discussing Mr. Keen Investor, we have made some assumptions (e.g., he is able to increase his savings by 20% each year, and he is aided at times by economic cycles). Suppose you cannot increase your savings each year by 20%, or that you are hindered rather than helped by economic conditions? The answer is simply that these things do not matter in long-term disciplined investing. Economic conditions may delay the achievement of financial freedom by a few years, but they have no power to stop you from reaching your goal. (Please note that these comments do not apply to short-term investing.)

Conversely, you may already have $7,000 or $8,000 to invest. In this case, you will be able to achieve your goal sooner.

Depending on your individual requirements, you may want to construct your investment blocks differently. No matter what you do, as long as you are disciplined, regular, and diversified in your investments, achieving financial freedom is a virtual certainty.

PART V
KEEPING TRACK OF YOUR PROGRESS

20

HOW TO START AND STAY ON COURSE

a. WATCHING YOUR PROGRESS

When you begin investing, your progress may not look very dramatic. For example, when you start investing $150 a month at 12%, at the end of the year you will have only about $100 more than you invested. If some investments go down temporarily, your return may look even worse. You may be tempted to give up your investment program. Don't. Remember this: Your investments always work slowly at the beginning. After a few years they gather momentum. It is important not to give up your program simply because it moves too slowly at the beginning.

As we saw earlier, money makes money and that money makes even more money. Suppose you stick with your investment program for a few years and accumulate $100,000. At this stage, the return on this amount would be $1,000 a month. But you cannot get there unless you are patient. If you follow the program outlined in this book, you will get there sooner or later.

There is another reason why your progress may seem slow. It is because you are too close to the action. It is like watching a child grow. If you attempt to watch a child grow every day, it is difficult to know how fast that child is growing. The change is gradual and is not even noticeable on an everyday basis.

In any case, it is important to keep track of your progress. Keeping track forces you to make regular investments and shows where your program's strengths and weaknesses are.

b. YOUR FINANCIAL FREEDOM WORKBOOK

You may want to consider the following format for creating your own "Financial Freedom Workbook":

(a) Buy a spiral notebook with ruled lines (8.5" x 11").

(b) On the first page, fill in the following information:

Your name:	*Mr. Keen Investor*
Amount you can save each day (or month):	*$150 per month*
Number of investments:	*8*
Type of investments:	*Stock Funds*
	Bond Funds
	Money Funds
	Gold Funds
	Foreign Funds
	Real Estate Funds

(Please note that these are just examples. Feel free to create your own investment programs and rules. Whatever you do, you should feel comfortable about your plan. For example, if you don't want to buy gold bullion or put your money in a Swiss bank, don't. Instead, buy something you are more comfortable with, such as stock market mutual funds. No matter what you decide, you should be determined to implement your plan.)

(c) Write down your investment plan.

Months	Amount	Investment
January/February	*$300*	*Stock Funds*
March/April	*300*	*Bond Funds*
May/June	*300*	*Money Market Funds*
July/August	*300*	*Gold Mutual Funds*
September/October	*300*	*Foreign Funds*
November/December	*300*	*Real Estate Funds*

(d) Write down any ideas you have that will help you achieve financial freedom faster:

I will save at least 50% of all windfalls such as bonuses, tax refunds, and pay increases.

If, in any given year, one of my investments rises in value by more than 30%, I'll sell about 20% and buy investments that have fallen in value.

(e) Use the Financial Freedom Worksheets (see Samples #1 and #2 on the following pages) as a model and create worksheets for your investments. You should have one worksheet for each type of investment. For example, Mr. Keen Investor puts $150 in stock market funds twice a year. The "Total value" column of your worksheet shows you how your investment is performing month after month. Keeping such records serves two purposes: first, it shows how your investment has been doing; second, it will come in handy during the tax season.

Over the years, you can create new worksheets to record your progress. This will be your "Financial Freedom Workbook."

In any case, you can start with the above and work through it for the first year. Then, you can modify the records to suit your purposes any way you like.

If you don't want to go to the trouble of creating your own record book, you can order your own "Financial Freedom Workbook" from the address below. This workbook comes with ready-to-use blank worksheets, as well as detailed instructions on how to record your program and a concise review of basic investment principles. Write to:

Standard Research Systems Inc.
26 Soho Street, Suite 380
Toronto, ON M5T 1Z7

SAMPLE #1
FINANCIAL FREEDOM WORKSHEET

MONTHLY WORKSHEET (USE A SEPARATE SHEET FOR EACH TYPE OF INVESTMENT)

INVESTMENT TYPE STOCK MARKET FUND

YEAR 1993

	Previous Investments	January	February	March	April	May	June
Amount Invested	—	$150					
Market Value	—	$150	$180	$185	$195	$189	$185
Dividends	/						
Interest	/						
Total	—	$150	$180	$185	$195	$189	$185

	July	August	Sept.	October	Nov.	Dec.	Year End
Amount invested	$150						$300
Market Value	$335	$355	$385	$395	$375	$365	$365
Dividends							
Interest							
Total	$335	$355	$385	$395	$375	$365	$365
Notes on							

Transfer this to the Year-end worksheet

SAMPLE #2
FINANCIAL FREEDOM
YEAR-END WORKSHEET

YEAR-END WORKSHEET

YEAR 1993   Carried forward from last year   1

		Investment Type					
	PREVIOUS INVESTMENTS	STOCK MKT. FUND	MONEY MKT. FUND	BOND FUND	FOREIGN FUND	REAL ESTATE FUND	GOLD FUND
Amount invested	1	$300	$300	$500	$300	$300	$300
Market Value	1	$365	$310	$340	$325	$250	$300
Dividends	1						
Interest	1						
Total	1	$365	$310	$340	$325	$250	$300

	Investment Type						
							Year end
Amount invested							$1,800
Market Value							$1,890
Dividends							
Interest							
Total							$1,890

Notes on   Gain During the Year $1,890 - $1,800 = $90

Transfer this to the 'previous investments' column for the next year.

One workbook has enough space to record details of your investments for several years. During this time I hope you will achieve financial freedom — or at least be very close to it!

PART VI
RESOURCE DIRECTORY

HOW TO KEEP YOURSELF INFORMED

This book has most of the information you need to start investing. But, to be a successful investor, you should keep yourself informed at all times.

a. USEFUL PUBLICATIONS

1. Investors Association of Canada: *Money Digest*

If you are following the strategy outlined in this book, it is necessary for you to be an informed investor. The Investors Association of Canada (IAC) publishes a newsletter 12 times a year. *Money Digest* lists the best performing mutual funds, high-quality dividend-paying stocks, GIC rates, etc., along with informative articles written by experts. (You can get a free copy of *Money Digest* by completing and sending in the comment sheet at the end of this book.) *Money Digest* is not available at newsstands and is distributed only to IAC members. I strongly recommend that you join the association. For more information, write to:

Money Digest
Investors Association of Canada
26 Soho Street, Suite 380
Toronto, ON M5T 1Z7

2. Daily publications (for serious investors)

United States

- *Wall Street Journal*

- The business section of any major daily newspaper such as the *New York Times*

Canada

- *Report on Business* (*Globe and Mail*)

- *Financial Post* (*National Post*)

3. Weekly publications

United States

- *Barron's*

4. Monthly publications

United States

- *Money*

Canada

- *MoneySaver* (11 times a year)

b. BOOKS

1. Investing in general

(a) For U.S. investors

- *Getting Started in Stocks* by Alvin D. Hall (3rd edition, published by John Wiley & Sons, 1997).

- *Learn to Earn: A Beginner's Guide to the Basics of Investing and Business* by Peter Lynch (with John Rothchild, contributor) (published by Fireside, 1996)

(b) For Canadian investors

- *Beginner's Guide to Investing* by Richard Croft and Eric Kirzner (published by HarperCollins Publishers, 1997). Gives the basics of investing and how to put your money to work for you.

- *Financial Pursuit* by Graydon Watters (published by FKI Financial Knowledge Inc., Toronto, revised 1996). An excellent book on financial planning.

- *How to Invest in Canadian Securities* (published by the Canadian Securities Institute, Toronto). A good introduction to investing in Canadian stock markets. Revised from time to time.

2. Mutual funds

(a) For U.S. investors

- *Business Week Guide to Mutual Funds* by Jeffrey Laderman (8th edition, 1998).

- *Getting Started in Mutual Funds* by Alan Lavine (published by John Wiley & Sons, 1994).

- *Low-Load Mutual Funds* (published annually by the Association of Individual Investors, Chicago).

- *New York Institute of Finance Guide to Investing in Mutual Funds* by Kirk Kazaryian.

(b) For Canadian investors

- *The Buyer's Guide to Mutual Funds* by Gordon Pape (published annually by Prentice Hall, Toronto). A fund-by-fund listing of all mutual funds offered in Canada.

- *Top Funds* by Riley Moynes and Michael Nairne (published annually by Addison Wesley Longman).

- *Understanding Mutual Funds* by Steven Kelman (published by Penguin Books, Toronto). A concise introduction to Canadian mutual funds. Revised yearly.

3. Gold

- *The ABCs of Gold Investing: Protecting Your Wealth Through Private Gold Ownership* by Michael J. Kosares (published by Addicus Books, 1997).

4. Options

- *Getting Started in Options* by Michael C. Thomsett (3rd edition, published by John Wiley & Sons, 1997).

- *Option Strategies* by Courtney D. Smith (2nd edition, published by John Wiley & Sons, 1996). One of the clearest introductions to various option strategies.

5. Real estate

- *Getting Started in Real Estate* by Michael C. Thomsett and Jean Freestone Thomsett (2nd edition, published by John Wiley & Sons, 1994)

- *Real Estate Investing from A to Z: The Most Comprehensive, Practical, and Readable Guide to Investing Profitably in Real Estate* by William H. Pivar (published by McGraw-Hill, 1997).

U.S. AND CANADIAN MUTUAL FUNDS

There are thousands of mutual funds in North America. Many hundreds of these are no-load funds (i.e., they charge no sales commission). *The funds listed here are no-load funds that require an initial minimum of no more than $500.* Once you become more familiar with mutual funds and increase your capital, you may want to explore other no-load funds that require a larger minimum. At that point, I suggest that you get information on other no-load funds by contacting other sources mentioned in this book.

In the following lists, "MIN" refers to the minimum investment required when you first join the fund; "SUB" refers to the minimum amount required if you subsequently want to add to your investment. All "1-800" and "1-888" numbers are toll free.

a. U.S.–BASED FUNDS

1. Aggressive growth funds

- Amer Cent 20th Century Gifttrust
  American Cent 20th Century
  4500 Main Street
  Box 419200
  Kansas City, MO 64141
  Phone: 1-800-345-2021/(816) 531-5575
  www.americancentury.com
  MIN: $500   SUB: $50

- Excelsior Small Cap A
  c/o Chase Global Fund Services Co.
  Box 2798
  Boston, MA 02208
  Phone: 1-800-446-1012
  MIN: $500   SUB: $50

- KEY Capital Growth
  KEY Funds
  45 Rockerfeller Plaza, 33rd Floor
  New York, NY 10111
  Phone: 1-800-539-3863/(212) 903-1200
  MIN: $500   SUB: $25

2. Growth funds

- API Trust: Growth for American Pension Investors — Growth
  Box 2529
  2303 Yorktown Avenue
  Lynchburg, VA 24501
  Phone: 1-800-544-6060/(804) 846-1361
  MIN: $500   SUB: $100

- Babson Growth
  Jones & Babson Distributors
  BMA Tower, 700 Karnes Boulevard
  Kansas, MO 64108
  Phone: 1-800-422-2766/(816) 471-5200
  www.jbfunds.com
  MIN: $500   SUB: $25

- Capstone Growth
  Capstone Financial
  5847 San Felipe, Suite 4100
  Houston, TX 77057-3011
  Phone: 1-800-262-6631/(713) 260-9000
  www.capstonefinancial.com
  MIN: $200   SUB: $1

- Excelsior Blended Equity
  Excelsior Value & Restructuring
  See address and phone number under
  U.S. aggressive growth fund section
  MIN: $500   SUB: $50

- Fairport Midwest Growth
  c/o Roulston & Co.
  4000 Chester Avenue
  Cleveland, OH 44103
  Phone: 1-800-332-6459/(216) 431-3000
  MIN: $250   SUB: $50

- KEY Fund
  See address and phone number under
  U.S. aggressive growth fund section
  MIN: $500   SUB: $25

- MSB Fund
  330 Madison Avenue
  New York, NY 10017
  Phone: (212) 551-1920
  MIN: $50   SUB: $25

- Nicholas
  Nicholas II
  700 N. Water Street, Suite 1010
  Milwaukee, WI 53202
  Phone: 1-800-227-5987/(414) 272-6133
  MIN: $500   SUB: $100

- Sentry
  1800 N. Point Drive
  Stevens Point, WI 54481
  Phone: 1-800-533-7827/(715) 346-7048
  MIN: $500   SUB: $50

3. Growth and income funds

- AARP Growth & Income
  c/o Scudder Funds
  Box 2291
  Boston, MA 02107-2291
  Phone: 1-800-253-2277/(617) 295-1000
  aarp.scudder.com
  MIN: $500   SUB: $1

- Aquinas Equity & Income
  5310 Harvest Hill Road, Suite 248
  Dallas, TX 75230
  Phone: (972) 233-6655
  MIN: $500   SUB: $250

- Century Shares Trust
  One Liberty Square
  Boston, MA 02109
  Phone: 1-800-321-1928/(617) 482-3060
  MIN: $500   SUB: $25

- Excelsior Growth & Income Fund
  See address and phone number under
  U.S. aggressive growth fund section
  MIN: $500   SUB: $50

- Homestead Value
  4301 Wilson Boulevard
  Arlington, VA 22203-1860
  Phone: 1-800-258-3030/(703) 907-6039
  www.nreca.org/homestead
  MIN:$500   SUB: $100

- KEY Convertibles Securities
  See address and phone number under
  U.S. aggressive growth fund section
  MIN: $500   SUB: $25

- Muhlenkamp Fund
  Muhlenkamp & Company
  12300 Perry Highway
  Wexford, PA 15090
  Phone: 1-800-539-3863/(212) 902-1200
  www.muhlenkamp.com
  MIN: $200   SUB: $100

- Strong Total Return
  Strong Funds Capital Management
  Box 2936
  Milwaukee, WI 53201
  Phone: 1-800-368-1030/(414) 359-3400
  www.strong-funds.com
  MIN: $250   SUB: $50

4. Balanced funds

- AARP Balanced Stock & Bond
  See address and phone number under
  growth and income fund section
  MIN: $500   SUB: $1

- Aquinas Balanced
  See address and phone number under
  growth and income fund section
  MIN: $500   SUB: $250

- PAX World
  222 State Street
  Portsmouth, NH 03801-3853
  Phone: 1-800-767-1729/(603) 431-8022
  www.paxfund.com
  MIN: $250   SUB: $50

- Strong Asset Allocation
  See address and phone number under
  growth and income fund section
  MIN: $250   SUB: $50

5. International stock funds

- Excelsior International
  Excelsior Latin America
  Excelsior Pacific Asia
  Excelsior Pan European
  See address and phone number under
  U.S. aggressive growth fund section
  MIN: $500   SUB: $50

b. CANADA-BASED FUNDS

1. Canadian equity funds (stock market funds)

- Associate Investors Ltd.
  Leon Frazer & Associates Ltd.
  8 E. King Street, Suite 2001
  Toronto, ON M5C 1B6
  Phone: (416) 864-1120
  Fax: (416) 864-1491
  MIN: $100   SUB: $100

- Batirente — Equity SSQ
  2525 blvd. Laurier
  Ste-Foy, QC G1V 4H5
  Phone: 1-800-361-8100
  Fax: (514) 288-4280
  MIN: $500   SUB: $500

- CDA Aggressive Equity (A)
  CDA Canadian Equity (T)
  CDA Common Stock (A)
  CDA Special Equity (K)
  CDA TSE 35 Index*
  Canadian Dental Association
  Retirement Savings Plan
  Canadian Dental Service Plans Inc.
  100 Consillium Place, Suite 710
  Scarborough, ON M1H 3G8
  Phone: 1-800-561-9401
  Fax: (416) 296-8920
  MIN: None   SUB: None   *MIN: $50

- Camaf
  Canadian Anaesthetists Mutual Fund Ltd.
  94 Cumberland Street, Suite 503
  Toronto, ON M5R 1A3
  Phone: 1-800-267-4713
  Fax: (416) 920-7843
  MIN: $500   SUB: $20

- Canada Trust — Special Equity
  Canada Trust Stock Fund
  CT Mutual Fund Services Inc.
  110 Yonge Street, 7th Floor
  Toronto, ON M5C 1T4
  Phone: 1-800-450-7311
  Fax: (416) 361-5333
  MIN: $500   SUB: None

- Canadian Imperial Equity
  CIBC Cdn. Small Companies
  CIBC Cdn. Emerging Co.
  CIBC Securities
  200 W. King Street, 7th Floor
  Toronto, ON M5H 4A8
  Phone: 1-800-465-3863
  Fax: (416) 351-4444
  MIN: $500   SUB: $25

- Co-Operators Canadian Equity
  Co-Operators Life Insurance
  1920 College Avenue
  Regina, SK S4P 1C4
  Phone: 1-800-604-0050
  Fax: (306) 347-6810
  MIN: $50   SUB: $50

- CSS Fonds Actions
  Caisse de Securitie du Spectacle
  3433 Stanley
  Montreal, QC H3A 1S2
  Phone: (514) 288-6682
  Fax: (514) 288-9364
  MIN: None   SUB: None

- Empire Equity Growth
  Empire Life Insurance Co.
  259 E. King Street
  Kingston, ON K7L 3A8
  Phone: (613) 548-1890
  Fax: (613) 548-4104
  MIN: None   SUB: None

- Ethical Special Equity
  Ethical Growth
  Credential Asset Mgmt. Inc.
  1441 Creekside Drive, 8th Floor
  Vancouver, BC V6J 4S7
  Phone: 1-877-384-4225
  Fax: (604) 714-3801
  MIN: $500   SUB: $100

- First Canadian Equity Index Fund
  First Canadian Growth Fund
  First Canadian Special Growth Fund
  Bank of Montreal Investment Management Ltd.
  First Canadian Mutual Funds
  302 Bay Street, 10th Floor
  Toronto, ON M5X 1A1
  Phone: 1-800-665-7700
  Fax: (416) 927-2710
  MIN: $500   SUB: $50

- GWL Canadian Equity (G) NL
  GWL Canadian Opportunity (M) NL
  GWL Equity (M) NL
  GWL Equity Fund (S) NL
  GWL Equity Index (G) NL
  GWL Growth Equity (M) NL
  GWL Larger Company (M) NL
  GWL Mid Cap Canada(G) NL
  GWL Smaller Company (M) NL
  Great-West Life Assurance Co.
  60 N. Osborne Street
  Winnipeg, MB R3C 3A5
  Phone: (204) 946-8622
  Fax: (204) 946-1190
  MIN: $50   SUB: $50

- Hongkong Bank Equity Fund
  Hongkong Bank Small Cap Growth
  Hongkong Bank Securities Inc.
  25th Oceanic Plaza, 1066 W. Hastings Street
  Vancouver, BC V6E 3X1
  Phone: 1-800-830-8888
  Fax: (604) 247-4867
  MIN: $500   SUB: $50

- InvesNat Cdn. Equity Fund
  InvesNat Cdn. Index Plus
  InvesNat Protected Cdn. Equity
  InvesNat Group of Funds
  c/o National Bank Securities Ltd.
  1100 University, 7th Floor
  Montreal, QC H3B 2G7
  Phone: (514) 394-9937
  Fax: (514) 394-8804
  MIN: $500   SUB: $50

- IRIS Canadian Equity Fund
  IRIS Small Cap Cdn. Equity
  IRIS Str Gro Opt Bal
  IRIS Str Inc Opt Bal
  IRIS Tactical Opt Bal
  IRIS Group of Funds
  850 Place d'Youville
  Quebec City, QC G1R 3P6
  Phone: 1-800-587-1221
  Fax: (418) 692-1675
  MIN: $500   SUB: $50

- Lotus Cdn. Equity
  Lotus Group of Funds
  1066 W. Hastings Street, Suite 2520
  Vancouver, BC V6E 3X1
  Phone: 1-800-665-9360
  Fax: (604) 669-8420
  MIN: $500   SUB: $50

- Manulife Cabot Blue Chip
  Manulife Cabot Cdn. Emerging Growth
  Manulife Cabot Cdn. Equity
  Manulife Cabot Cdn. Growth
  Manulife Cabot Series
  500 N. King Street
  Waterloo, ON N2J 4C6
  Phone: 1-800-265-7401
  Fax: 1-800-265-5123
  MIN: $500   SUB: $500

- Mutual Alpine Equity
  Mutual Premier Blue Chip Fund
  Mutual Premier Growth Fund
  Mutual Summit Equity
  Mutual Summit Gro & Inc
  The Mutual Group
  c/o Mutual Diversico Ltd.
  227 S. King Street
  Waterloo, ON N2J 4C5
  Phone: 1-888-564-5463
  Fax: (519) 888-3480
  MIN: $500   SUB: $50

158

- National Trust Cdn. Index*
  National Trust Equity Fund
  National Trust Special Equity
  National Trust
  1 E. Adelaide Street
  Toronto, ON M5C 2W8
  Phone: 1-800-563-4684
  Fax: (416) 361-5563
  MIN: $500   SUB: $50   *MIN & SUB: None

- OIQ Ferique — Equity
  OIQ — Growth
  OIQ Ferique
  c/o Ordre des Ingenieurs du Quebec
  2020 University, 18th Floor
  Montreal, QC H3A 2A5
  Phone: 1-800-261-6141
  Fax: (514) 845-1833
  MIN: $500   SUB: None

- OTG Investment Fund — Diversified
  OTG Investment Fund — Growth
  Ontario Teachers Group
  57 Mobile Drive
  Toronto, ON M4A 1H5
  Phone: 1-800-263-9541
  Fax: (416) 752-6649
  MIN: $500   SUB: $50

- PH&N Vintage Fund
  Phillips, Hager & North Management Ltd.
  200 Burrard Street, 21st Floor
  Vancouver, BC V6C 3N5
  Phone: 1-800-661-6141
  Fax: (604) 685-5712
  MIN: None   SUB: None

- Scotia Excel Cdn. Bluechip
  Scotia Excel Cdn. Growth
  Scotia Excelsior Mutual Funds
  40 W. King Street, 5th Floor
  Toronto, ON M5H 1H1
  Phone: 1-800-268-9269
  Fax: (416) 266-4455
  MIN: $500   SUB: $25

- Transamerica Agent Plan
  Transamerica Life Insurance Co. of Canada
  300 Consilium Place
  Scarborough, ON M1H 3G2
  Phone: 1-800-758-1634
  Fax: (416) 290-2896
  MIN: None   SUB: None

- Westbury Canadian Life Equity
  Westbury Canadian Life
  Box 298, 21 W. King Street
  Hamilton, ON L8N 3R5
  Phone: 1-800-263-9241
  Fax: (905) 526-3100
  MIN: $30   SUB: $30

2. **U.S. equity funds**

- Canada Trust AmeriGrowth
  Canada Trust US Equity
  See address and phone number under
  Canadian equity funds section
  MIN: $500   SUB: None

- Co-Operators US Equity
  See address and phone number under
  Canadian equity funds section
  MIN: $50   SUB: $50

- Ethical NA Equity
  See address and phone number under
  Canadian equity funds section
  MIN: $500   SUB: $100

- First Canadian Equity Index
  First Canadian Special Growth
  First Canadian US Growth Fund
  First Canadian Value
  See address and phone number under
  Canadian equity funds section
  MIN: $500   SUB: $50

- GWL Amer Growth (A) NL
  GWL US Equity (G) NL
  See address and phone number under
  Canadian equity funds section
  MIN: $50   SUB: $50

- Hongkong Bank US Equity
  See address and phone number under
  Canadian equity funds section
  MIN: $500   SUB: $50

- Ind Alliance US Stock
  Ind Alliance US Adv U
  See address and phone number under
  Canadian equity funds section
  MIN: None   SUB: None

- IRIS US Equity Fund
  See address and phone number under
  Canadian equity funds section
  MIN: None   SUB: None

- InvesNat American Index Plus
  See address and phone number under
  Canadian equity funds section
  MIN: $500   SUB: $50

- Mutual Premier American Fund
  See address and phone number under
  Canadian equity funds section
  MIN: $500   SUB: $50

- National Trust American Equity Fund
  National Trust US Index*
  See address and phone number under
  Canadian equity funds section
  MIN: $500   SUB: $50   *MIN & SUB: None

161

- OIQ Ferique American
  See address and phone number under
  Canadian equity funds section
  MIN: $500   SUB: None

- Scotia Excel American Growth
  Scotia CanAm Growth Fund
  See address and phone number under
  Canadian equity funds section
  MIN: $500   SUB: $25

3. International equity funds

- AGF Germany Class M
  AGF Management
  TD Tower, Suite 3100, Box 50
  Toronto, ON M5K 1E9
  Phone: 1-800-520-0620
  Fax: (416) 865-4197
  MIN: None   SUB: None

- Canada Trust Asia Growth
  Canada Trust Emerging Mkts.
  Canada Trust EuroGrowth
  Canada Trust Global Growth
  Canada Trust Intl. Equity
  See address and phone number under
  Canadian equity funds section
  MIN: None   SUB: None

- CDA Emerging Markets
  CDA European (KBSH)
  CDA Global Fund
  See address and phone number under
  Canadian equity funds section
  MIN: None   SUB: None

- CDA Global Stock (TE)
  CDA International Equity (K)
  CDA Pacific Basin (KBSH)
  See address and phone number under
  Canadian equity funds section
  MIN: $50   SUB: $25

- CIBC International Index
  CIBC Int Index RRSP Fund
  CIBC Intl. Small Co. Fund
  CIBC Latin American
  CIBC NA Demographics
  See address and phone number under
  Canadian equity funds section
  MIN: $500   SUB: $25

- Ethical Pacific Rim
  See address and phone number under
  Canadian equity funds section
  MIN: $500   SUB: $100

- First Cdn. International Growth Fund
  First Cdn. Latin America
  First Cdn. Emerg Markets
  First Cdn. European Growth
  First Cdn. Far East Growth
  First Cdn. Glo Sci & Tech
  First Cdn. Japanese Growth
  First Cdn. NAFTA Advantage
  See address and phone number under
  Canadian equity funds section
  MIN: $500   SUB: $50

- FMOQ International Equity
  Fed. des Medecins Omnipracticiens
  1440 Ste-Catherine O., Suite 1012
  Montreal, QC H3G 1R8
  Phone: 1-888-542-8597
  Fax: (514) 868-2088
  MIN: $500   SUB: $100

- GWL Asian Growth (A) NL
  GWL Euro Equity (S) NL
  GWL Intl. Oppor (P) NL
  GWL Intl. Equity (P) NL
  GWL NA Equity (B) NL
  See address and phone number under
  Canadian equity funds section
  MIN: $50   SUB: $50

163

- Hongkong Bank Asian Growth Fund
  Hongkong Bank Emerg Mkts
  Hongkong Bank Euro Growth
  Hongkong Global Equity
  See address and phone number under
  Canadian equity funds section
  MIN: $500   SUB: $50

- Ind Alliance Emerg Mkts
  Ind Alliance International Fund
  See address and phone number under
  Canadian equity funds section
  MIN: None   SUB: None

- InvesNat European Equity Fund
  InvesNat Far East Equity
  InvesNat Japanese Equity
  InvesNat Protected Intl.
  See address and phone number under
  Canadian equity funds section
  MIN: $500   SUB: $50

- IRIS Global Equity Fund
  See address and phone number under
  Canadian equity funds section
  MIN: $500   SUB: $100

- Manulife Cabot Glo Equity
  See address and phone number under
  Canadian equity funds section
  MIN: $500   SUB: $500

- Millennia NA Sml Co Ser 2
  Imperial Life Assurance
  Millennia III Plan
  95 W. St. Clair Avenue
  Toronto, ON M4V 1N7
  Phone: 1-800-278-0669
  Fax: (416) 926-2907
  MIN: $500   SUB: $50

- Mutual Alpine Asian Fund
  Mutual Premier Emerging
  Mutual Premier International Fund
  Mutual Summit Foreign Equity
  See address and phone number under
  Canadian equity funds section
  MIN: $500   SUB: $50

- National Trust Emerging Markets
  National Trust International Equity
  See address and phone number under
  Canadian equity funds section
  MIN: $500   SUB: $500

- OIQ Ferique International
  See address and phone number under
  Canadian equity funds section
  MIN: $500   SUB: $50

- OTG Investment Global Value
  See address and phone number under
  Canadian equity funds section
  MIN: $500   SUB: $50

- PH&N Global Equity Trust
  See address and phone number under
  Canadian equity funds section
  MIN: None   SUB: None

- Scotia Excel Euro Growth
  Scotia Excel Intl.
  Scotia Excel Latin America
  Scotia Excel Pacific Rim
  See address and phone number under
  Canadian equity funds section
  MIN: $500   SUB: $50

4. Specialty equity funds

- Centerfire Growth Fund
  Centerfire Investment Mgmt.
  141 W. Adelaide Street, Suite 277
  Toronto, ON M5H 3L9
  Phone: 1-888-777-2949
  Fax: (416) 777-0706
  MIN: $500   SUB: $50

- Crocus Investment Fund
  275 Broadway, Suite 303
  Winnipeg, MB R3C 4M6
  Phone: (204) 925-2401
  Fax: (204) 942-2785
  MIN: $250   SUB: None

- ENSIS Growth Fund (LSVCC)
  ENSIS Growth Fund
  c/o BPI Mutual Funds
  161 Bay Street, Suite 3900
  Toronto, ON M5J 2S1
  Phone: 1-800-263-2427
  Fax: (416) 861-9415
  MIN: $500   SUB: $50

- First Cdn. Precious Metals
  First Cdn. Resource Fund
  See address and phone number under
  Canadian equity funds section
  MIN: $500   SUB: $50

- First Ontario Fund (LSVCC)
  First Ontario Fund
  234 W. Eglinton Avenue, Suite 310
  Toronto, ON M4P 1K5
  Phone: 1-800-777-7506
  Fax: (416) 487-1345
  MIN: $500   SUB: $50

- GWL Canadian Resources (A) NL
  See address and phone number under
  Canadian equity funds section
  MIN: $50   SUB: $50

- Innovacap Capital Corp.
  Box 2034, Station D
  Ottawa, ON K1P 5W3
  Phone: 1-888-843-7777
  Fax: (613) 230-3531
  MIN: $500   SUB: $500

- Mutual Alpine Resources
  See address and phone number under
  Canadian equity funds section
  MIN: $50   SUB: $50

- Scotia Precious Metals Fund
  See address and phone number under
  Canadian equity funds section
  MIN: $500 SUB: $25

- Triax Growth Fund (LSVCC)
  Triax Capital Management
  BCE Place
  161 Bay Street, Suite 4700
  Toronto, ON M5J 2S1
  Phone: 1-800-407-0287
  Fax: (416) 362-2199
  MIN: $500   SUB: $50

- Working Opportunity EVCC
  Working Opportunity Fund
  Box 11170, Royal Centre
  1055 W. Georgia Street, Suite 2901
  Vancouver, BC V6E 3R5
  Phone: (604) 688-9631
  Fax: (604) 669-7605
  MIN: $500   SUB: $25

5. Balanced funds

- APM Balanced
  c/o Trustco Desjardins
  1 Complexe Desjardins, Box 34
  Montreal, QC H5B 1E4
  Phone: (514) 286-3225
  Fax: (514) 849-3328
  MIN: $100   SUB: None

- Barreau Quebec Balanced
  Cormel Funds
  Barreau du Quebec
  c/o Fiducie Desjardins
  1 Complexe Desjardins, 15th Floor
  Montreal, QC H5B 1E4
  Phone: (514) 286-3100
  Fax: (514) 286-5457
  MIN: None   SUB: None

- Batirente — Diversified
  See address and phone number under
  Canadian equity funds section
  MIN: $500   SUB: $500

- CDA RSP Balanced Fund
  See address and phone number under
  Canadian equity funds section
  MIN: None   SUB: None

- Canada Trust Balanced
  Canada Trust Balanced Ind
  Canada Trust Glo Asst Allocation
  Canada Trust Ret Balanced
  See address and phone number under
  Canadian equity funds section
  MIN: $500   SUB: None

- Co-Operators Balanced
  Co-Operators US Diversified
  See address and phone number under
  Canadian equity funds section
  MIN: $50   SUB: $50

- CSFPQ Balanced
  c/o Trustco Desjardins
  1 Complexe Desjardins, Box 34
  Montreal, QC H5B 1E4
  Phone: (514) 286-5948
  Fax: (514) 286-3328
  MIN: $100   SUB: None

- CSS Fonds Equilibre
  See address and phone number under
  Canadian equity funds section
  MIN: None   SUB: None

- Ethical Balanced
  See address and phone number under
  Canadian equity funds section
  MIN: $500   SUB: $100

- First Cdn. Asset Allocation Fund
  See address and phone number under
  Canadian equity funds section
  MIN: $500   SUB: $50

- FMOQ Fonds de Placement
  FMOQ Omnibus Balanced
  FMOQ Investment
  See address and phone number under
  Canadian equity funds section
  MIN: $500   SUB: $100

- GWL Advanced Port (G) NL
  GWL Aggr Port (G) NL
  GWL Balanced Fund (B) NL
  GWL Balanced Fund (M) NL
  GWL Balanced Fund (S) NL
  GWL Balanced Port (G) NL
  GWL Conserv Port (G) NL
  GWL Diversified (G) NL
  GWL Equity/Bond (G) NL
  GWL Growth & Inc (A) NL
  GWL Growth & Inc (M) NL
  GWL Income Invest (G) NL
  GWL Moderate Port (G) NL
  See address and phone number under
  Canadian equity funds section
  MIN: $50   SUB: $50

- Hongkong Bank Balanced Fund
  See address and phone number under
  Canadian equity funds section
  MIN: $500   SUB: $50

- Ind Alliance Diversified DNL
  Ind Alliance Diversified S-2
  Ind Alliance Diversified
  See address and phone number under
  Canadian equity funds section
  MIN: None   SUB: None

- InvesNat Protected Grow Balanced
  InvesNat Protected Ret Balanced
  InvesNat Retirement Balanced Fund
  See address and phone number under
  Canadian equity funds section
  MIN: $500   SUB: $50

- IRIS Balanced Fund
  See address and phone number under
  Canadian equity funds section
  MIN: $500   SUB: $50

- Lotus Balanced Fund
  See address and phone number under
  Canadian equity funds section
  MIN: $500   SUB: $50

- Members Mutual Fund
  Members Mutual Management Corp.
  55 E. Lakeshore Boulevard
  Toronto, ON M5E 1A4
  Phone: 1-888-560-2218
  Fax: (416) 864-6858
  MIN: $200   SUB: $50

- Mutual Premier Diversified
  See address and phone number under
  Canadian equity funds section
  MIN: $500   SUB: $50

- National Trust Balanced Fund
  See address and phone number under
  Canadian equity funds section
  MIN: $500   SUB: $50

- OIQ Ferique Balanced
  See address and phone number under
  Canadian equity funds section
  MIN: $500   SUB: None

- OTG Balanced Fund
  See address and phone number under
  Canadian equity funds section
  MIN: $500   SUB: $50

- Remec Equilibre
  Corp. Maitre Mecaniciens en Teyanterie
  c/o Desjardins Trust
  1 Complexe Desjardins, 15th Floor
  Montreal, QC H5B 1E4
  Phone: (514) 286-3225
  Fax: (514) 849-3329
  MIN: None   SUB: None

- Royal Trust Advantage Growth Fund
  See address and phone number under
  Canadian equity funds section
  MIN: $500   SUB: $25

- Scotia Excel Balanced for Scotia Stock & Bond Fund
  Scotia Excel Total Return
  See address and phone number under
  Canadian equity funds section
  MIN: $500   SUB: $25

- Westbury Cdn. Life Balanced
  See address and phone number under
  Canadian equity funds section
  MIN: $30   SUB: $30

6. Preferred dividend funds

- Canada Trust Dividend Inc.
  See address and phone number under
  Canadian equity funds section
  MIN: $500   SUB: None

- First Cdn. Dividend Income
  See address and phone number under
  Canadian equity funds section
  MIN: $500   SUB: $50

- GWL Div/Growth (M) NL
  GWL Dividend (G) NL
  See address and phone number under
  Canadian equity funds section
  MIN: $50   SUB: $50

- Hongkong Bank Div Income
  See address and phone number under
  Canadian equity funds section
  MIN: $500   SUB: $50

- Ind Alliance Dividend V
  See address and phone number under
  Canadian equity funds section
  MIN: None   SUB: None

- InvesNat Dividend
  See address and phone number under
  Canadian equity funds section
  MIN: $500   SUB: $50

- IRIS Dividend Fund
  See address and phone number under
  Canadian equity funds section
  MIN: $500   SUB: $50

- Millennia Cdn. Div Ser 2
  See address and phone number under
  International equity funds section
  MIN: $500   SUB: $50

- Mutual Summit Div Growth
  See address and phone number under
  Canadian equity funds section
  MIN: $500   SUB: $50

- National Trust Dividend Fund
  See address and phone number under
  Canadian equity funds section
  MIN: $500   SUB: $50

- Scotia Excel Dividend
  See address and phone number under
  Canadian equity funds section
  MIN: $500   SUB: $25

7. Mortgage funds

- Canada Trust Mortgage
  See address and phone number under
  Canadian equity funds section
  MIN: $500   SUB: None

- First Canadian Mortgage Fund
  See address and phone number under
  Canadian equity funds section
  MIN: $500   SUB: $50

- GWL Mortgage
  See address and phone number under
  Canadian equity funds section
  MIN: $50   SUB: $50

- Ind Alliance Mortgages
  See address and phone number under
  Canadian equity funds section
  MIN: None   SUB: None

- InvesNat Mortgage Fund
  See address and phone number under
  Canadian equity funds section
  MIN: $500   SUB: $50

- IRIS Mortgage Fund
  See address and phone number under
  Canadian equity funds section
  MIN: $500   SUB: $50

- Mutual Premier Mortgage Fund
  See address and phone number under
  Canadian equity funds section
  MIN: $500   SUB: $50

- National Trust Mortgage
  See address and phone number under
  Canadian equity funds section
  MIN: $500   SUB: $50

- OTG Investment Mortgage Income Fund
  See address and phone number under
  Canadian equity funds section
  MIN: $500   SUB: $50

173

- Scotia Excel Mortgage Fund
  See address and phone number under
  Canadian equity funds section
  MIN: $500   SUB: $25

8. Bond/mortgage funds

- Barreau Quebec Bond
  See addresses and phone number under
  Canadian balanced funds
  MIN: None   SUB: None

- CDA RSP Bond & Mortgage Funds
  See address and phone number under
  Canadian equity funds section
  MIN: None   SUB: None

- Scotia Excel Income Fund
  See address and phone number under
  Canadian equity funds section
  MIN: $500   SUB: $25

c. BOND FUNDS (U.S.)

1. Corporate high-yield bond funds

- Nicholas Income
  See address and phone number under
  growth funds section
  MIN: $500   SUB: $100

2. Mortgage-backed bond funds

- AARP GNMA & US Treasury
  See address and phone number under
  growth funds section
  MIN: $500   SUB: $1

3. General bond funds

- Aquinas Fixed Income
  See address and phone number under
  U.S. growth and income funds section
  MIN: $500   SUB: $250

- Babson Bond Trust — Port L
  Babson Bond Trust — Port S
  See address and phone number under
  growth and income funds
  MIN: $500   SUB: $50

- Excelsior Interm-Term Managed Income
  Excelsior Managed Income
  See address and phone number under
  U.S. aggressive growth funds section
  MIN: $500   SUB: $50

- Homestead Short-Term Bond
  See address and phone number under
  U.S. growth and income funds section
  MIN: $500   SUB: $100

4. Tax-exempt bond funds

- Dupree KY Tax-Free Income
  Dupree KY Tax-Free Short to Medium
  P.O. Box 1149
  Lexington, KY 40588-1149
  Phone: 1-800-866-0614 / (606) 254-7741
  www.dupree-funds.com
  MIN: $100   SUB: $100

- Excelsior Interm-Term Tax Exempt
  Excelsior Long-Term Tax Exempt
  Excelsior NY Interm Tax Exempt
  See address and phone number under
  U.S. aggressive growth funds section
  MIN: $500   SUB: $50

d. BOND FUNDS (CANADIAN)

- Barreau Quebec Bond
  See address and phone number under
  balanced funds section
  MIN: None   SUB: None

- Batirent Bond
  See address and phone number under
  Canadian equity funds section
  MIN: $500   SUB: $500

- Canada Trust Bond Fund
  Canada Trust International Bond
  Canada Trust Short Term Bond
  See address and phone number under
  Canadian equity funds section
  MIN: $500   SUB: None

- CDA Fixed Income (MB)
  See address and phone number under
  Canadian equity funds section
  MIN: None   SUB: None

- CIBC Canadian Bond Index
  CIBC Global Bond Index
  See address and phone number under
  Canadian equity funds section
  MIN: $500   SUB: $25

- Co-Operators Fixed Income
  See address and phone number under
  Canadian equity funds section
  MIN: $50   SUB: $50

- CSS Fonds Obligataire
  See address and phone number under
  Canadian equity funds section
  MIN: None   SUB: None

- Ethical Global Bond
  Ethical Bond
  See address and phone number under
  Canadian equity funds section
  MIN: $500   SUB: $100

- First Canadian Bond Fund
  First Canadian International Bond Fund
  See address and phone number under
  Canadian equity funds section
  MIN: $500   SUB: $50

- FMOQ Bond
  See address and phone number under
  International equity funds section
  MIN: $500   SUB: $100

- GWL Bond (B) NL
  GWL Bond (S) NL
  GWL Cdn. Bond (G) NL
  GWL Global Income (A) NL
  GWL Govt. Bond (G) NL
  GWL Income (M) NL
  GWL International Bond (P) NL
  See address and phone number under
  Canadian equity funds section
  MIN: $50   SUB: $50

- Hongkong Bank Canadian Bond
  Hongkong Bank Global Bond
  See address and phone number under
  Canadian equity funds section
  MIN: $500   SUB: $50

- Ind Alliance Bond BNL
  Ind Alliance Bonds S-2
  Ind Alliance Global Bond
  Ind Alliance Income R
  See address and phone number under
  Canadian equity funds section
  MIN: None   SUB: None

- InvesNat Short-Term Government Bond Fund
  InvesNat International RSP Bond
  InvesNat Protected Cdn. Bond
  See address and phone number under
  Canadian equity funds section
  MIN: $500   SUB: $50

- IRIS Bond Fund
  IRIS NA High Yield Bond
  See address and phone number under
  Canadian equity funds section
  MIN: $500   SUB: $50

- Lotus bond
  See address and phone number under
  Canadian equity funds section
  MIN: $500   SUB: $50

- Manulife Cabot Diversified Bond
  See address and phone number under
  Canadian equity funds section
  MIN: $500   SUB: $50

- Mutual Premier Bond Fund
  See address and phone number under
  Canadian equity funds section
  MIN: $500   SUB: $50

- National Trust Canadian Bond
  National Trust International RSP Bond
  See address and phone number under
  Canadian equity funds section
  MIN: $500   SUB: $50

- OIQ Ferique Bond Fund
  See address and phone number under
  Canadian equity funds section
  MIN: $500   SUB: None

- Scotia CanAm Income Fund
  Scotia Defensive Income Fund
  Scotia Excel Global Bond
  See address and phone number under
  Canadian equity funds section
  MIN: $500   SUB: $25

- Westbury Canadian Life Bond
  See address and phone number under
  Canadian equity funds section
  MIN: $30   SUB: $30

e. MONEY MARKET FUNDS (U.S.)

I have not included a listing of money market fund addresses for the U.S. as the number of funds is too high. Please consult your local newspaper or financial institution for more information.

f. MONEY MARKET FUNDS (CANADIAN)

- Acadia Money Market
  Acadia Investment Funds
  294 W. St. Pierre Boulevard
  Caraquet, NB E1W 1B7
  Phone: 1-800-351-1345
  Fax: (506) 724-4025
  MIN: $500   SUB: $50

- Atlas Canadian Money Market
  Atlas Asset Management
  20 Bay Street, Suite 1402
  Toronto, ON M5J 2N8
  Phone: 1-800-263-2857
  Fax: (416) 943-5916
  www.atlasfunds.ca
  MIN: $500   SUB: $500

- Batirente — Section Marche Monetaire
  See address and phone number under
  Canadian equity funds section
  MIN: $500   SUB: $500

- CDA RSP Money Market Fund
  See address and phone number under
  Canadian equity funds section
  MIN: $50   SUB: $50

- Co-Operators Money Market Fund
  See address and phone number under
  Canadian equity funds section
  MIN: $50   SUB: $50

- Colonial Money Market Fund
  Colonial Life Insurance Company
  2 E. St. Clair Avenue
  Toronto, ON M4T 2V6
  Phone: 1-800-463-9297
  Fax: 1-800-405-1206
  MIN: $500   SUB: $100

- Ethical Money Market
  See address and phone number under
  Canadian equity funds section
  MIN: $500   SUB: $100

- Ficadre Astra — MM
  Ficadre Funds
  625 rue Sainte-Amable
  Quebec, QC G1R 2G5
  Phone: (418) 644-4225
  Fax: (418) 528-0457
  MIN: $500   SUB: $50

- FMOQ Marche Monetaire
  See address and phone number under
  Canadian equity funds section
  MIN: $500   SUB: $100

- First Canadian Money Market Fund
  First Canadian T-Bill Fund
  See address and phone number under
  Canadian equity funds section
  MIN: $500   SUB: $50

- Fonds Astra
  SSQ Societe d'assurance-vie Inc.
  2525 blvd. Laurier, Box 10510
  Ste-Foy, QC G1V 4H5
  Phone: (418) 688-4887
  Fax: (418) 688-7791
  MIN: $400   SUB: $400

- GWL Money Market (G) NL
  See address and phone number under
  Canadian equity funds section
  MIN: $50   SUB: $50

- Hongkong Bank Money Market
  See address and phone number under
  Canadian equity funds section
  MIN: $500   SUB: $500

- Ind Alliance Money Market Fund
  See address and phone number under
  Canadian equity funds section
  MIN: None   SUB: None

- Lotus Income Fund
  See address and phone number under
  Canadian equity funds section
  MIN: $500   SUB: $50

- Manulife Cabot MMF
  See address and phone number under
  Canadian equity funds section
  MIN: $500   SUB: $500

- Maxxum Money Market
  Maxxum Group
  33 Yonge Street, Suite 810
  Toronto, ON M5E 1G4
  Phone: 1-888-462-9986
  Fax: 1-888-629-9861
  www.maxxum.funds
  MIN: $500   SUB: $300

- Mutual Money Market Fund
  See address and phone number under
  Canadian equity funds section
  MIN: $500   SUB: $50

- National Trust Money Market Fund
  See address and phone number under
  Canadian equity funds section
  MIN: $500   SUB: $50

- O'Donnell Money Market
  O'Donnell Fund Management
  4100 Yonge Street, Suite 610
  Toronto, ON M2P 2B5
  Phone: 1-800-292-5658
  Fax: (416) 221-5200
  MIN: $500   SUB: $100

- OIQ Ferique — Marche Monetaire
  See address and phone number under
  Canadian equity funds section
  MIN: $500   SUB: $50

- OTG Investment Fund — Fixed Value Section
  See address and phone number under
  Canadian equity funds section
  MIN: $500   SUB: $50

- Spectrum United Savings Fund
  Spectrum United Services
  145 W. King Street, Suite 300
  Toronto, ON M5H 1J8
  Phone: 1-800-404-2227
  Fax: (416) 352-3200
  MIN: $500   SUB: $30

g. DISCOUNT BROKERS

The following is a list of discount stockbrokers in the United States and Canada.

1. United States

- Accutrade
  4211 S. 102nd Street
  Omaha, NE 68127
  Phone: 1-800-228-3011
  www.accutrade.com

- Advisors Group
  51 Louisiana Avenue N.W.
  Washington, DC 20001
  Phone: 1-800-999-3699

- AGS Financial Services
  208 LaSalle Street, Suite 2059
  Chicago, IL 60604
  Phone: 1-800-436-0705

- American Express Financial Direct
  Box 59195
  Minneapolis, MN 55459-0196
  www.americanexpress.com/direct

- Andrew Pack Associates
  111 Pavonia Avenue
  Jersey City, NJ 07310
  Phone: 1-800-221-5873
  www.thehost.com/peck

- Arnold Securities
  830 S. Second Avenue
  Minneapolis, MN 55402
  Phone: 1-800-328-4076

- Aufhauser & Company
  112 W. 56th Street
  New York, NY 10019
  Phone: 1-800-368-3668
  www.aufhauser.com

- Baker & Company
  1940 E. Sixth Street
  Cleveland, OH 44114
  Phone: 1-800-223-2638
  www.bakernyse.com

- Bank of San Francisco Brokerage Services
  550 Montgomery Street
  San Francisco, CA 94111
  Phone: 1-800-338-3965

- Barry Murphy & Company
  77 Summer Street
  Boston, MA 02110
  Phone: 1-800-221-2111

- Berlind & Company
  1 North Broadway
  White Plains, NY 10601
  Phone: (914) 761-6665

- Bidwell
  209 Oak Street S.W.
  Portland, OR 97204
  Phone: 1-800-547-6337
  www.bidwell.com

- Brown & Company
  20 Winthrop Square
  Boston, MA 02110
  Phone: 1-800-822-2021

- Bruno, Stolze & Company
  12444 Powerscourt Drive, Suite 230
  St. Louis, MO 63131
  Phone: (314) 821-1990

- Bull & Bear Securities
  11 Hanover Square
  New York, NY 10005
  Phone: 1-800-262-5800

- Burke, Christensen & Lewis
  303 Madison Street
  Chicago, IL 60606
  Phone: 1-800-621-0392

- Ceres Securities
  Box 3288
  Omaha, NE 68103-9964
  Phone: 1-800-669-3900
  www.ceres.com

- Charles Schwab
  101 Montgomery Street
  San Francisco, CA 94104
  Phone: 1-800-435-4000
  www.schwab.com

- CompuTEL Securities
  1 Second Street, 5th Floor
  San Francisco, CA 94105
  Phone: 1-800-432-0327
  www.rapidtrade.com

- Consolidated Financial Investments
  287 N. Lindbergh, Suite 201
  St. Louis, MO 63141
  Phone: 1-800-292-6637

- Corby North Bridge Securities
  99 Bedford Street
  Boston, MA 02111
  Phone: 1-800-736-7076
  www.northbridge.com

- Datek Securities
  50 Broad Street, 6th Floor
  New York, NY 10004
  Phone: 1-888-GODATEK
  www.datek.com

- DLJ*direct*Inc.
  1 Pershing Plaza
  Jersey City, NJ 07399
  Phone: 1-800-825-5723
  www.dljdirect.com

- Downstate Discount Brokers
  259 N. Indian Rocks Road
  Belleair Bluffs, FL 34640
  Phone: 1-800-780-3543

- eBroker
  Box 2226
  Omaha, NE 68103-2226
  www.ebroker.com

- Empire Financial Group
  220 Crown Oak Center Drive
  Longwood, FL 32750
  Phone: 1-800-900-8101
  www.iag.net/empire/

- E*Trade
  2400 Geng Road
  Palo Alto, CA 94303
  Phone: 1-800-786-2575
  www.etrade.com

- Fidelity Investments
  161 Devonshire Street
  Boston, MA 02110
  Phone: 1-800-544-8666
  www.341.fidelity.com

- First Union Brokerage Services
  301 S. College Street, 5th Floor
  Charlotte, NC 28288
  Phone: 1-800-326-4434
  www.firstunion.com

- Fleet Brokerage
  150 Winsor MSN 223
  Box 5408
  Hartford, CT 06101-8204
  Phone: 1-800-766-3000

- Freedom Investments
  11422 Miracle Hills Drive, Suite 501
  Omaha, NE 68154
  Phone: 1-800-381-1481
  www.tradeflash.com

- Freeman Welwod & Company
  1501 Fourth Avenue, Suite 1700
  Seattle, WA 98101
  Phone: 1-800-729-7585

- GIT Discount Brokerage
  1700 N. Moore Street
  Arlington, VA 22209
  Phone: 1-800-336-3063
  www.presidential.com/prototype/broker.html

- Icahn & Company
  90 S. Bedford Road
  Mt. Kisco, NY 10549
  Phone: 1-800-634-8518

- Investors National Corporation
  1300 N. State Street
  Bellingham, WA 98227
  Phone: 1-800-728-1266
  www.saturna.com/inc/INC.html

- Jack White & Company
  9191 Towne Centre Drive, Suite 220
  San Diego, CA 92122
  Phone: 1-800-233-3411
  www.pawws.com/jwc

- J.B. Oxford & Company
  9665 Wilshire Boulevard, Suite 300
  Beverly Hills, CA 90212
  Phone: 1-800-500-5007
  www.jboxford.com

- J.D. Siebert
  20 W. Ninth Street
  Cincinnati, OH 45202
  Phone: 1-800-247-3396

- John Finn & Company
  205 Dixie Terminal Building
  Cincinnati, OH 45202
  Phone: 1-800-743-7059

- Kashner Davidson Securities
  77 S. Palm Avenue
  Sarasota, FL 34236
  Phone: 1-800-678-2626

- Kennedy, Cabot & Company
  9470 Wilshire Boulevard
  Beverly Hills, CA 90212
  Phone: 1-800-252-0090

- Levitt & Levitt
  135 LaSalle Street, Suite 1945
  Chicago, IL 60603-4303
  Phone: 1-800-671-8505

- Lombard Institutional Brokerage
  595 Market Street
  San Francisco, CA 94105
  Phone: 1-800-566-2273
  www.lombard.com

- MarQuette De Bary Company
  488 Madison Avenue
  New York, NY 10022
  Phone: 1-800-221-3305
  www.debary.com

- Marsh Block & Company
  50 Broad Street
  New York, NY 10004
  Phone: (212) 514-6400

- Max Ule
  26 Broadway, Suite 200
  New York, NY 10004
  Phone: 1-800-223-6642
  www.maxule.com

- Mongerson & Company
  135 S. LaSalle Street, Suite 2147
  Chicago, IL 60603-4109
  Phone: 1-800-621-2627

- Muriel Siebert & Company
  885 Third Avenue, Suite 1720
  New York, NY 10022
  Phone: 1-800-872-0711

- National Discount Brokers
  50 Broadway, 18th Floor
  New York, NY 10004
  Phone: 1-800-888-3999
  pawws.secapl.com/ndb

- Net Investor
  Phone: 1-800-638-4250
  pawws.secapl.com/invest.html

- OLDE Discount Stockbrokers
  751 Griswold Street
  Detroit, MI 48226
  Phone: 1-800-872-6533
  www.oldediscount.com

- Pacific Brokerage Services
  5757 Wilshire Boulevard, Suite 3
  Los Angeles, CA 90036
  Phone: 1-800-421-8395
  www.tradepbs.com

- Pacific Continental Securities
  8484 Wilshire Boulevard, Suite 744
  Beverly Hills, CA 90211
  Phone: 1-800-367-9829
  www.pcos.com

- Peremel & Company
  1829 Reistertown Road, Suite 120
  Baltimore, MD 21208
  Phone: 1-800-666-1440

- Prestige Status
  603 Grand Central Parkway, Suite 271
  Floral Park, NY 11005
  Phone: 1-800-782-8871

- Principal Financial Securities
  2 N. LaSalle Street
  Chicago, IL 60602-3702
  Phone: 1-800-621-4480

- PT Discount Brokerage
  11 S. LaSalle Street, Suite 1500
  Chicago, IL 60603
  Phone: 1-800-248-5008
  www.ptdiscount.com

- Quick & Reilly
  26 Broadway
  New York, NY 10004
  Phone: 1-800-221-5220
  www.quick-reilly.com

- Recom Securities
  619 S. Marquette Avenue, Suite 142
  Minneapolis, MN 55402
  Phone: 1-800-328-8600

- Regal Discount Securities
  209 W. Jackson Boulevard, 4th Floor
  Chicago, IL 60606
  Phone: 1-800-786-9000
  www.regaldiscount.com

- R.F. Lafferty & Company
  50 Broad Street
  New York, NY 10004
  Phone: 1-800-221-8514

- R.J. Forbes Group
  150 Broad Hollow Road
  Melville, NY 11747
  Phone: 1-800-488-0090
  www.rjforbes.com

- Rodecker & Company
  4000 Town Center
  Southfield, MI 48075
  Phone: 1-800-676-1848

- Royal Grimm & Davis
  17 Battery Place
  New York, NY 10004
  Phone: (212) 943-7960

- Russo Securities
  128 Sand Lane
  Staten Island, NY 10305
  Phone: 1-800-451-7877

- S.C. Costa Company
  320 S. Boston Avenue, West Lobby
  Tulsa, OK 74103
  Phone: (918) 582-0110

- Savoy Discount Brokerage
  823 Third Avenue, Suite 206
  Seattle, WA 98104-1617
  Phone: 1-800-961-1500
  www.savoystocks.com

- Scottsdale Securities
  12855 Flushing Meadow Drive
  St. Louis, MO 63131
  Phone: 1-800-888-1980
  www.discountbroker.com

- Seaport Securities Corporation
  19 Rector Street
  New York, NY 10006
  Phone: 1-800-732-7678

- Securities Research
  936-A Beachland Boulevard, Suite 202
  Vero Beach, FL 32963
  Phone: 1-800-327-3156

- Shearman Ralston
  17 Battery Place, Suite 604
  New York, NY 10004-1102
  Phone: 1-800-221-4242

- Shochet Securities
  1484 E. Hallandale Beach Boulevard
  Hallandale, FL 33009
  Phone: 1-800-327-1536

- Spectrum Securities
  6800 Owensmouth, Suite 340
  Canoga Park, CA 91303
  Phone: 1-800-779-2355

- St. Louis Discount Securities
  200 S. Hanley, Lobby Suite 103
  Clayton, MO 63105
  Phone: 1-800-726-7401

- State Discount Brokers
  27600 Chargrin Boulevard
  Cleveland, OH 44122
  Phone: 1-800-222-5520
  www.state-discount.com

- Sterling Investment Services
  135 S. LaSalle Street, Suite 720
  Chicago, IL 60603
  Phone: 1-800-782-1522

- Stockcross
  1 Washington Mall
  Boston, MA 02108
  Phone: 1-800-225-6196

- The Stock Mart
  12655 Beatrice Street
  Los Angeles, CA 90066
  Phone: 1-800-421-6563

- Summit Discount Brokerage
  305 Route 17 S.
  Parmaus, NY 07652
  Phone: 1-800-631-1635

- T. Rowe Price Discount Brokerage
  100 E. Pratt Avenue
  Baltimore, MD 21202
  Phone: 1-800-225-7720
  www.troweprice.com/brokerage/brokerage.html

- Tradex Brokerage Service
  20 Vesey Street
  New York, NY 10007
  Phone: 1-800-522-3000

- Tuttle Securities
  307 S. Townsend Street
  Syracuse, NY 13202
  Phone: 1-800-962-5489

- USAA Brokerage Services
  USAA Building
  San Antonio, TX 78288
  Phone: 1-800-531-8343

- The Vanguard Group
  Vanguard Financial Center
  Valley Forge, PA 19496-9906
  Phone: 1-800-992-8327
  www.vanguard.com/vbs/VBSHome.cgi

- Voss & Company
  6225 Brandon Avenue
  Springfield, VA 22150
  Phone: 1-800-426-8106

- Wall Street Access
  17 Battery Place
  New York, NY 10004
  Phone: 1-800-487-2339
  www.wsaccess.com

- The Wall Street Discount Corporation
  100 Wall Street
  New York, NY 10005
  Phone: 1-800-221-7870
  www.wsdc.com

- Wall Street Equities
  40 Exchange Place
  New York, NY 10005
  Phone: 1-800-447-8625

- Washington Discount Brokerage
  100 Wall Street
  New York, NY 10005
  Phone: 1-800-843-9601

- Waterhouse Securities
  100 Wall Street
  New York, NY 10005
  Phone: 1-800-934-4430
  www.waterhouse.com

- White Discount Securities
  1 Second Street, 5th Floor
  San Francisco, CA 94105
  Phone: 1-800-432-0327
  www.wdsonline.com

- Wisconsin Discount Securities
  7161 N. Port Washington Road
  Milwaukee, WI 53217
  Phone: 1-800-537-0239

- W.J. Gallagher & Company
  2920 Garfield, Suite 303
  Missoula, MT 59801
  Phone: 1-800-935-6633

- York Securities
  160 Broadway, East Building, 7th Floor
  New York, NY 10038
  Phone: 1-800-221-3154

- Young, Stovall & Company
  9627 S. Dixie Highway, Suite 101
  Miami, FL 33156
  Phone: 1-800-433-5132

- Your Discount Broker
  855 S. Federal Highway
  Boca Raton, FL 33432
  Phone: 1-800-800-3215

- Ziegler Thrift Trading
  733 Marquette Avenue, Suite 106
  Minneapolis, MN 55402-2340
  Phone: 1-800-328-4854
  www.ziegler-thrift.com

2. Canada

- Affinity Investments
  40 University Avenue
  Toronto, ON M5J 1T1
  Phone: (416) 585-9690
  www.affinity.ca

- Bank of Montreal Investor Services
  First Canadian Place
  100 W. King Street, 20th Floor
  Toronto, ON M5X 1A1
  Phone: 1-800-387-7800
  www.investorline.com

- CIBC Investors Edge
  200 W. King Street, 16th Floor
  Toronto, ON M5H 4A8
  Phone: 1-800-567-3343
  www.cibc.com

- CT Market Partner
  Phone: 1-800-530-9000
  www.ctsecurities.com

- E*Trade
  181 Bay Street, Suite 3810
  Toronto, ON M5J 2T3
  Phone: 1-888-872-3383
  www.etrade.com

- Hongkong Bank Discount Trading
  70 York Street, Suite 1680
  Toronto, ON M5J 1S9
  Phone: (416) 868-8000
  www.hkbc.com/english/ibro_ooo.html

- Royal Bank Action Direct
  200 Bay Street, Royal Bank Plaza
  Toronto, ON M5J 2J5
  Phone: (416) 974-7493
  www.royalbank.com

- Scotia Discount Brokerage
  1 W. Richmond Street, 7th Floor
  Toronto, ON M5H 3W2
  Phone: 1-800-263-3430
  www.sdbi.com

- TD Green Line Investor Services
  55 King Street, Concourse Level
  Toronto, ON M5K 1A2
  Phone: (416) 982-7981
  www.tdbank.ca

h. NORTH AMERICAN STOCK EXCHANGES

The following is a list of North American stock and commodity exchanges.

1. United States

- American Stock Exchange (AMEX)
  86 Trinity Place
  New York, NY 10006-1881
  Phone: 1-800-THE-AMEX/(212) 306-1000
  www.amex.com

- Arizona Stock Exchange
  200 N. Central Avenue, Suite 1230
  Phoenix, AZ 85004
  Phone: (602) 222-5858
  www.azx.com

- Boston Stock Exchange (BSE)
  1 Boston Place
  Boston, MA 02108
  Phone: (617) 723-9500
  www.bostonstock.com

- Chicago Board of Trade (CBOT)
  141 W. Jackson Boulevard
  Chicago, IL 60604-2994
  Phone: (312) 435-3500
  www.cbot.com

- Chicago Board Options Exchange (CBOE)
  400 S. LaSalle Street
  Chicago, IL 60605
  Phone: (312) 786-5600
  www.cboe.com

- Chicago Mercantile Exchange (CME)
  30 S. Wacker Drive
  Chicago, IL 60606
  Phone: (312) 930-1000
  www.cmr.com

- Chicago Stock Exchange
  440 S. LaSalle Street
  Chicago, IL 60605
  Phone: (312) 663-2980
  www.chicagostockex.com

- Cincinnati Stock Exchange (CSE)
  440 S. LaSalle Street, 26th Floor
  Cincinnati, OH 45202
  Phone: (312) 939-7239

- Coffee, Sugar & Cocoa Exchange (CSCE)
  4 World Trade Center
  New York, NY 10048
  Phone: (212) 938-2900
  www.csce.com

- Kansas Board of Trade (KCBT)
  4800 Main Street, Suite 303
  Kansas City, MO 64112
  Phone: (816) 812-5228
  www.kcbt.com

- MidAmerica Commodity Exchange (MIDAM)
  141 W. Jackson Boulevard
  Chicago, IL 60604
  Phone: (312) 341-3000/(312) 341-3078
  www.midam.com

- Minneapolis Grain Exchange (MGE)
  400 S. Fourth Street
  130 Grain Ex. Building
  Minneapolis, MN 55415-1413
  Phone: 1-800-827-4746
  www.mgex.com

- NASDAQ Stock Market
  1735 K Street N.W.
  Washington, DC 20006-1500
  Phone: (202) 728-8840

- New York Cotton Exchange (NYCE)
  4 World Trade Center, Suite 5572
  New York, NY 10048
  Phone: 1-800-692-6886/(212) 742 5050

- New York Futures Exchange (NYFE)
  Phone: (212) 938-4940

- New York Mercantile Exchange (NYMEX)
  1 N. End Avenue
  World Financial Center
  New York, NY 10282-1101
  Phone: (212) 299-2000
  www.nymex.com

- New York Stock Exchange (NYSE)
  11 Wall Street
  New York, NY 10005
  Phone: (212) 656-3000
  www.nyse.com

- Pacific Stock Exchange (PSE)
  301 Pine Street
  San Francisco, CA 94104
  Phone: (415) 393-4000
  pacificex.com

- Philadelphia Stock Exchange (PHLS)
  Philadelphia Board of Trade (PBOT)
  1900 Market Street
  Philadelphia, PA 19103
  Phone: (215) 496-5102

2. Canada

- Alberta Stock Exchange
  300 Fifth Avenue S.W., 10th Floor
  Calgary, AB T2P 3C4
  Phone: (403) 974-7400
  www.alberta.net

- Montreal Exchange
  800 Square Victoria, Box 61
  Montreal, QC H4Z 1A9
  Phone: 1-800-361-5353
  www.me.org

- Toronto Futures Exchange
  Toronto Stock Exchange
  The Exchange Tower
  2 First Canadian Place
  Toronto, ON M5X 1J2
  Phone: (416) 947-4700/(416) 947-4487
  www.tse.com

- Vancouver Stock Exchange
  Stock Exchange Tower
  Box 10333, 609 Granville Street
  Vancouver, BC V7Y 1H1
  Phone: (604) 689-3334
  www.vse.com

- Winnipeg Commodity Exchange
  500 Commodity Exchange Tower
  360 Main Street
  Winnipeg, MB R3C 3Z4
  Phone: (204) 925-5000

- Winnipeg Stock Exchange
  1 Lombard Place, Suite 620
  Winnipeg, MB R3B 0X3
  Phone: (204) 987-7070
  www.wse.com

i. SWISS BANKS

The following is a list of Swiss banks. Please note that many of these banks need a large minimum. If you are curious, you may want to call or write to some of these banks and request more information.

- Bank Leu AG
  Bahnhofstrasse 32,8001
  Zurich Postfach CH-8022
  Switzerland 41 1219-1111
  www.bankleu.ch

- Credit Suisse
  Phone: 41 (844) 800-844
  www.en.credit-suisse.ch

- UBS AG
  G6399-RGF, Box P.O. 8098
  Zurich, Switzerland
  www.ubs.com

GET A FREE COPY OF *MONEY DIGEST*

We would like to know what you think of *Financial Freedom on $5 a Day*. We would appreciate it very much if you would take a few minutes to fill in this short comment sheet.

In return for your efforts, we will send you — absolutely free — the latest issue of *Money Digest*.

PLEASE PRINT

Your name_____Date_____

Address_____

City_____

State/Province_____ Postal code_____

Do you wish to be on our mailing list?   Yes_____ No_____

Can we quote your comments?   Yes_____ No_____

What investments interest you? _____

_____

_____

Please write your comments on the following page and mail to:

Standard Research Systems Inc.
26 Soho Street, Suite 380
Toronto, ON M5T 1Z7
Canada